Iraq

Iraq

BY NEL YOMTOV

Enchantment of the World™
Second Series

CHILDREN'S PRESS®

Frontispiece: **Shatt al-Arab**

Consultant: Harith Hasan Al-Qarawee, PhD, Research Fellow at the Central European University, Budapest, Hungary, and Non-Resident Fellow at Brandeis University, Waltham, Massachusetts

Please note: All statistics are as up-to-date as possible at the time of publication.

Book production by The Design Lab

Library of Congress Cataloging-in-Publication Data
Names: Yomtov, Nel, author.
Title: Iraq / by Nel Yomtov.
Description: New York, NY : Children's Press, an imprint of Scholastic Inc., 2018. | Series:
    Enchantment of the world | Includes bibliographical references and index.
Identifiers: LCCN 2017025777 | ISBN 9780531235904 (library binding)
Subjects: LCSH: Iraq—Juvenile literature.
Classification: LCC DS70.62 .Y66 2018 | DDC 956.7—dc23
LC record available at https://lccn.loc.gov/2017025777

Scholastic Inc., 557 Broadway, New York, NY 10012

1 2 3 4 5 6 7 8 9 10 R 27 26 25 24 23 22 21 20 19 18

Tea shop in Arbil

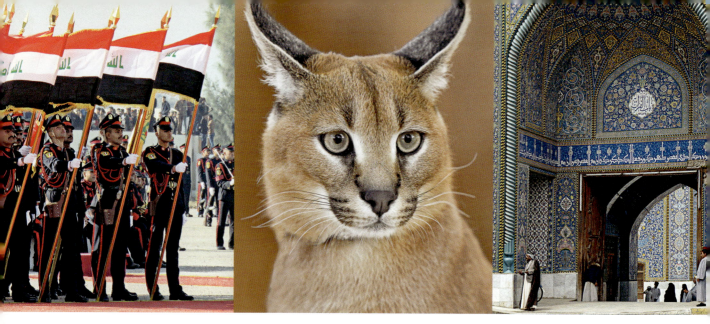

Contents

Left to right: **Army cadets, caracal, mosque, farmer, elderly man**

CHAPTER 1

A Nation at the Crossroads

THE LAND THAT IS NOW IRAQ WAS THE SITE OF humankind's first great civilizations and the birthplace of technologies that spawned brilliant cultures. Known as Mesopotamia—"the land between the rivers" in ancient Greek—it was here that writing, agriculture, mathematics, laws, government, and literature began. The two rivers are the Tigris and the Euphrates. Their life-giving waters provided rich soil for farming and water to irrigate crops. The rivers also supplied a means of transportation, which helped large-scale trade networks develop.

Opposite: **This bronze head of a bull dates back to the Sumerian culture about four thousand years ago.**

The great ancient city of Babylon, which appears in the Bible and has been studied extensively by archaeologists, lay in Mesopotamia. Known for its splendid buildings and artworks, the city was the region's dominant center of learning, culture, and commerce.

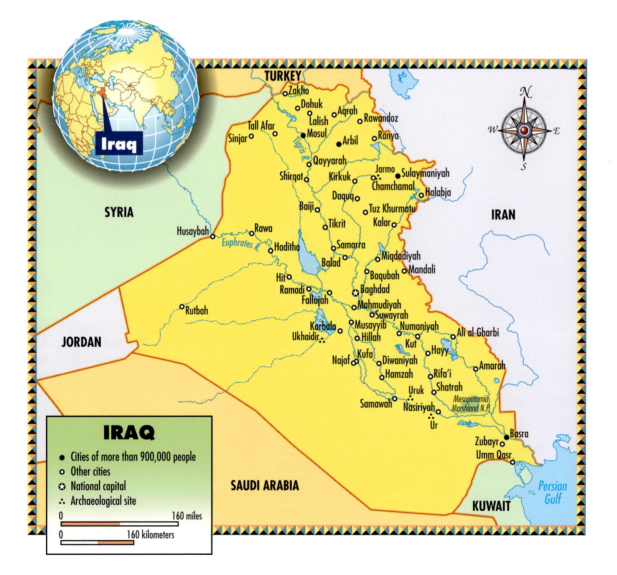

IRAQ

- ● Cities of more than 900,000 people
- ○ Other cities
- ⊕ National capital
- ∴ Archaeological site

0   160 miles

0   160 kilometers

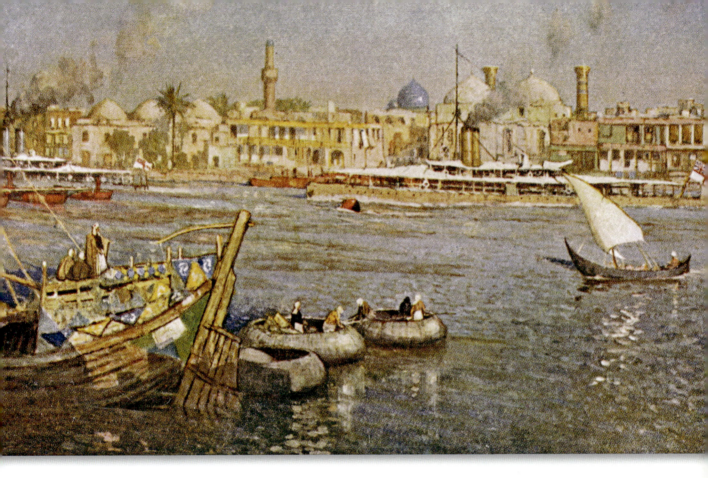

In later centuries, the city of Baghdad emerged as one of the world's greatest cities, a wealthy and influential center of Arab and Islamic culture.

The modern nation of Iraq came into existence only about a century ago. The discovery of oil in Iraq in 1927 propelled the young nation to international importance, making it a significant force in world politics and global economics. Iraq is a key oil producer, and this resource has greatly influenced its complex history. In recent decades, Iraqi people have relied on their resilience to overcome the many hardships they have faced, including invasions by foreign powers, uprisings, terrorist attacks, civil wars, and brutal dictatorships.

In the early twentieth century, Baghdad was a thriving city, home to more than 150,000 people.

Today, Iraq—a land that has been home to both remarkable civilizations and terrible destruction—is at a crossroads. Iraq's challenges are many. Access to health services is not yet available to all areas of the country, unemployment is high, and in some regions there are food and water shortages. Although the nation now has a democratically elected government, divisive politics have created tensions between Iraqi communities. In the past, religious or ethnic characteristics did not prevent peaceful coexistence, trade, and marriage among all groups. Today, however, fundamentalist groups

Girls play on a building destroyed during the Iraq War in 2003.

have been using terrorist violence to force Iraqi people to live in hatred and fear.

Iraq has the potential to return the nation to the glory of its past. Proper management of the country's vast oil reserves can make Iraq one of the wealthiest nations on the planet. With the help of international organizations, Iraqi institutions could be reformed and a promising economic environment could emerge, providing opportunities to invest in Iraq's reconstruction, agriculture, health care, and other sectors.

Above all, Iraq's greatest asset is the Iraqi people. Iraqis are strong and resilient, proud of their cultural heritage and the diversity of their nation. They remain determined to rebuild their country and create a brighter future for all generations to come.

Iraqi students relax on a beautiful day in Arbil, in the northern part of the country. Iraq's population is young. Nearly three out of five people in the country are under age twenty-five.

CHAPTER 2

Land Between the Rivers

I RAQ IS LOCATED IN SOUTHWESTERN ASIA IN A REGION known as the Middle East. Its neighbors are Turkey to the north; Iran to the east; Kuwait to the south; and Saudi Arabia, Jordan, and Syria to the west. Iraq covers 169,235 square miles (438,317 square kilometers), making it slightly larger than the state of California.

Iraq is almost entirely surrounded by land. Its only coastline is a small stretch at its southeastern corner where it touches the Persian Gulf.

Opposite: **The Euphrates River cuts across central Iraq. In some places, the desert begins just beyond its banks.**

Iraq's Geographic Features

Area: 169,235 square miles (438,317 sq km)

Highest Elevation: Cheekha Dar, 11,847 feet (3,611 m) above sea level

Lowest Elevation: Persian Gulf at sea level

Longest River: Euphrates River, about 720 miles (1,160 km) in Iraq

Largest Lake: Lake Tharthar (artificial), 965 square miles (2,500 sq km)

Longest Border: With Iran, 906 miles (1,458 km)

Shortest Border: With Jordan, 112 miles (180 km)

Largest City: Baghdad, population 7,216,000

Average Daily High Temperature: In Baghdad, 60°F (15.5°C) in January, 111°F (44°C) in July

Average Daily Low Temperature: In Baghdad, 39°F (4°C) in January, 74°F (23°C) in July

Highest Recorded Temperature: 129°F (54°C), in Basra, July 22, 2016

Lowest Recorded Temperature: 22°F (-6°C), in Baghdad

Average Annual Precipitation: 4 to 7 inches (10 to 18 cm); 2 feet (0.6 m) in mountainous regions

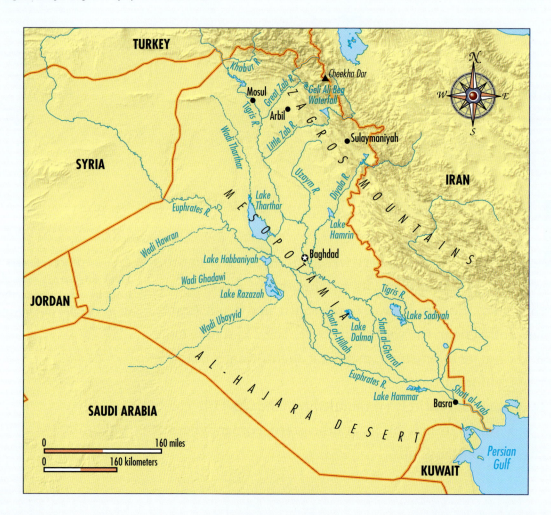

The Great Rivers

Iraq's most prominent geographical feature is its two major rivers, the Tigris and the Euphrates. For thousands of years, the rivers have been the economic backbone of Iraq.

Both rivers originate in the mountains of eastern Turkey and flow through northern Syria before reaching Iraq. The Euphrates is Iraq's longest river, measuring about 1,740 miles (2,800 km) in total length, of which about 720 miles (1,160 km) are in Iraq. It has no tributaries. The 1,180-mile-long (1,900 km) Tigris River is fed by several rivers flowing from the Zagros Mountains, the largest mountain range in Iraq and southeastern Turkey.

Only 25 miles (40 km) separate the Tigris and the Euphrates when they enter Iraq. As the two rivers flow southward, the valley between them broadens to as much as 250

On a hot day in Baghdad, young people cool off by diving into the Tigris River.

A cargo ship dwarfs small boats on the Shatt al-Arab, near Basra.

miles (400 km) across. During Iraq's rainy season each spring, the waters of the Tigris and Euphrates overflow. The floods carry rich soil into the river valleys to create fertile farmlands and provide water for crop irrigation.

The two rivers meet in southeastern Iraq, about 70 miles (113 km) north of the Persian Gulf near Basra. Here they form the waterway known as the Shatt al-Arab, which flows into the gulf. The Shatt al-Arab forms part of Iraq's border with Iran and provides an excellent link to the interior of Iraq. Ships from the Persian Gulf can travel up Shatt al-Arab to the Tigris and then farther north to the capital city of Baghdad in central Iraq.

The People of the Wetlands

For more than 6,000 years, the Marsh Arabs, also known as the Madan, lived in the southern marshlands of Iraq near the Iranian border. Living in a world of water and surrounded by thick vegetation, the Marsh Arabs remained largely isolated from their Iraqi neighbors. They built homes of reeds that grew in the area's marshlands. They often erected the homes on artificial islands also made of reeds. The marshes provided their inhabitants with fish, birds, lizards, wild boars, and other animals used for food. The Marsh Arabs made their living by fishing, herding water buffalo, and weaving reed mats.

In recent years, the ancient Marsh Arab way of life has become extinct. In the 1990s, the marshlands became a stronghold for rebellion against the regime of Iraq's dictator, Saddam Hussein. In response, Hussein

had engineers divert the Tigris and Euphrates Rivers away from the marshes to punish this population. The region was nearly turned into a desert, forcing about half a million Marsh Arabs to abandon their homes. The draining of the swamps was both an environmental crime and a human rights abuse.

Hussein was ousted from power in 2003. Since then, international groups have worked to restore the marshes and the wildlife that disappeared with the loss of the natural habitat. In 2013, Iraq announced the creation of its first national park, Mesopotamia Marshland National Park, which includes the southern marshes. There are no inhabited villages in the park because the people who fled their homes have established new lives for themselves elsewhere in Iraq. Hopes are that the once-lost culture will someday be able to return to its ancestral homeland.

The Zagros Mountains tower over a village in northeastern Iraq. In many places, the mountains serve as a border between Iraq and Iran.

A Varied Terrain

Iraq's varied physical landscape features tall mountains, flat plains, arid deserts, and a fertile delta.

The northeastern mountainous region includes the Zagros Mountains that begin north of the Iraqi cities of Mosul and Kirkuk and run into Iran and Turkey. This area features Iraq's most beautiful scenery, including lilac-covered mountainsides, golden grasses, and breathtaking waterfalls. The Zagros is home to Cheekha Dar, Iraq's tallest peak at 11,847 feet (3,611 meters) above sea level. Many other peaks in the Zagros top 9,000 feet (2,740 m). This region is populated mainly by Kurds, Iraq's largest non-Arab group.

Iraq's central plain region is divided into northern and southern sections. The dry northern plain lies between the Tigris and Euphrates northwest of Samarra. Tall hills, rolling grasslands, and small streams dot the landscape. The region's deep, dry valleys are difficult to irrigate, and little farming is done there. The southern plain stretches from Samarra to the Persian Gulf. This section includes the fertile delta at the mouth of the two great rivers. Most of Iraq's population lives in the southern plain, including the people who live in large cities such as Basra.

Nearly 40 percent of Iraq is desert. Desert regions are found in western and southwestern Iraq. The land is flat and rocky, with occasional rises of sand dunes and limestone hills. The enormous Syrian Desert extends westward into Syria, Jordan, and Saudi Arabia. The Al-Hajara Desert lies in the southwest and stretches into Saudi Arabia.

Narrow riverbeds called wadis crisscross the deserts. Most of the year the wadis are dry. During winter rainfalls, the channels fill with water to become rapidly moving rivers that flood the desert floor. The floodwaters bring on short-lived vegetation, which quickly disappears when winter ends.

Though desert regions remain largely unpopulated, the Al-Hajara Desert is home to nomadic groups such as the Bedouin. These Iraqi herders make their living by raising sheep and goats. They move from place to place with their animals, collecting water from local wadis.

Iraq's Climate

Iraq's climate, like its landscape, varies from region to region. The hottest areas are the arid deserts and southern plains. Temperatures in the deserts can reach a blazing 120 degrees Fahrenheit (49 degrees Celsius) in the summer, which runs from

Young Iraqis have a snowball fight in northern Iraq. Winters in this region are cold.

May to October. Summers are also harsh in the southern plains where average high temperatures in Baghdad hover around 111°F (44°C). Winters are comparatively mild in Baghdad, however, with average lows of about 39°F (4°C) in January.

The mountainous northeast has wet and cold winters. Temperatures average between 24°F and 63°F (–4°C and 17°C), but temperatures in the low teens are often recorded. Summers in the northwest are comfortable.

Iraq is mainly dry with sparse rainfall. Mountain regions receive between 12 and 20 inches (30 and 50 centimeters) of rain annually, but years of 40 inches (100 cm) are not uncommon. Much of the precipitation in the mountains comes in the form of snow. Springtime melting of snow in the higher elevations often causes widespread flooding in central Iraq. Annual rainfall in the delta is about 16 inches (41 cm). The desert receives little rainfall, averaging only 4 to 7 inches a year (10 to 18 cm).

Looking at Iraq's Cities

Baghdad, the capital of Iraq, is also its largest city, with an estimated population of 7,216,000 in 2017. Basra (below), Iraq's main port and second-largest city, has a population of 2,600,000. Located about 75 miles (120 km) from the Persian Gulf, ships travel the Shatt al-Arab waterway to reach Basra's port. Basra's economy is centered on Iraq's oil industry. Most of the country's oil exports ship from Basra. Several refining companies are located within the city. Fertile land surrounds Basra, where rice, barley, wheat, and dates are grown.

Mosul, Iraq's third-largest city with a population of 1,739,800, lies on the banks of the Tigris River in northern Iraq. The city is on the site of the ancient Assyrian city of Nineveh. For much of its history, Mosul was famed for its metalwork. Today, it is vital to the oil industry. Mosul is a diverse city, home to a rich mix of Arabs, Kurds, Assyrians, Turkmen, and others.

The city of Arbil (above), Iraq's fourth-largest city, has a population of roughly 932,800. Human presence at Arbil dates back seven thousand years, making it one of the world's oldest continuously inhabited places. Traditionally, Arbil was an important center for trade. It was a key junction on the pathway connecting the Persian Gulf to what is now Turkey, in the north. Today, Arbil is the capital of Iraq's province of Kurdistan, home of the Kurds, the largest ethnic group in the region. An ethnically diverse city, Arbil's population also includes Assyrians, Arabs, Armenians, and others. The city's oldest buildings lie in the Citadel of Arbil, which occupies a huge, high mound in the city center.

Land Between the Rivers **23**

CHAPTER 3

The Natural World

IRAQ IS HOME TO A WIDE RANGE OF PLANTS AND animals that have adapted to the country's various landscapes and climates. Many species thrive in the delta and temperate mountain region. Hardy wildlife survives with little water in the vast, dry deserts.

Opposite: **The caracal is one of several cat species that live in Iraq. They are easily identified by their tall, black tufted ears. In fact, their name comes from two Turkish words meaning "black ear."**

Mammals

Iraq is home to about ninety species of wild mammals. Most are small creatures, such as hedgehogs, shrews, badgers, porcupines, squirrels, and gerbils. Small cats live throughout Iraq.

Rebuilding the Zoo

The Baghdad Zoo, the largest zoo in the Middle East, was destroyed during the 2003 invasion of Iraq. Only 35 of the zoo's 650 animals survived the first week of the war. Animals were caught in the crossfire during fighting in the city. Many escaped and others roamed the zoo grounds where they died of hunger. Some animals were stolen by looters who sold or ate the animals.

Since then, U.S. military personnel and Iraqi citizens and officials have helped rebuild the zoo. Today, the zoo is open to the public and serves as home to more than a thousand animals, including Bengal tigers, ostriches, hyenas, cheetahs, and a rare white lion. Millions of people visit the zoo each year.

The sand cat inhabits the desert and arid southwest regions. The wildcat and lynx live in forested and wooded areas in the extreme north. Iraq also has about twenty species of bats. Among the larger mammals are goats, gazelles, camels, deer, wild boar, wolves, and foxes. The red fox lives around marshes, deserts, and the dry plains of central and southern Iraq. Rüppell's fox lives only in the western and southwestern deserts. Leopards, though rare, and brown bears are found in the forested mountains in the extreme north. Cheetahs once lived in several places throughout the country but are now probably extinct.

Dolphins, porpoises, blue whales, and humpback whales live off the coast of southern Iraq in the Persian Gulf. Otters are found in lakes, streams, and the marshes of the Tigris and Euphrates Rivers.

The black-crowned night heron lives near rivers, lakes, and marshes, and uses its heavy, pointed bill to snatch fish from the water.

In the Skies

About 415 species of birds make their home in Iraq, though many are short-term visitors that make annual migrations from colder regions in the north to the warmth of Iraq to breed. A number of birds of prey live in mountainous areas. These include eagles, hawks, falcons, vultures, and owls. Pheasants, gulls, sandpipers, owls, larks, pigeons, and storks are also frequent sights.

One common bird of Iraq is the black-crowned night heron. This squat, stocky bird is active at night or at dusk. Another bird, the ferruginous duck, is one of nearly thirty species of duck found in Iraq. It lives there year-round and feeds on water plants, insects, and small fish.

The greater flamingo, found in streams and in the marshes of southern Iraq, is the world's largest species of flamingo.

The National Bird

The chukar partridge is the national bird of Iraq. The chukar has light brown, gray, and yellow-white feathers. It bears distinctive black and white bars on the sides and a black band around the face and neck. Measuring up to 14 inches (36 cm) long, the bird is named for its sharp, noisy call—a chuck-chuck-chukar sound, which it repeats rapidly. The chukar feeds mostly on the ground, eating seeds, leaves, and grasses. Sometimes it moves into shrubs and trees for berries and insects.

These beautiful birds have pinkish-white feathers and a bright pink bill with a black tip. Greater flamingos have lived up to sixty years in captivity.

Fish, Amphibians, and Reptiles

About 140 species of freshwater fish live in Iraq's streams, rivers, and lakes. Catfish, pike, perch, herring, and eel are often caught as food. Carp caught in the waters of the Tigris River are seasoned and grilled, and served as *masgouf*, a favorite dish in Iraq. Though rare, the bull shark occasionally enters fresh waters from the Persian Gulf and travels up the Shatt al-Arab as far north as Baghdad.

About ten species of amphibians make Iraq their home. These include the spadefoot, a small toad with a shovel-like growth on its hind feet. The toad uses the "spades" to dig burrows in the ground in which it stays during the day. At night, the spadefoot emerges to feed on insects.

Dozens of types of reptiles are found throughout Iraq. Turtles, tortoises, terrapins, geckos, and a wide variety of lizards are common in both the north and the south. The short-nosed desert lizard lives in hot, arid habitats. Snakes are less common in Iraq, though some can be deadly. The bites of the Levantine viper and the saw-scaled viper are extremely deadly, capable of killing humans and large animals.

Plant Life

Few plants can survive in Iraq's dry, hot desert regions. Due to its long, deep roots, orchard grass grows year-round in drought conditions. The summer rains of December to April give rise to a variety of low-growing plants such as Jericho rose, milfoil, and tamarisk. After the rainy season, the plants scatter their seeds and dry up under the hot sun.

The marshlands and the riverbanks of the Tigris and Euphrates provide a more welcoming environment for plant life. Thickets of bulrushes and other grasses as well as willows and poplars are found along the banks of the great rivers. Licorice plants also flourish near the rivers. The roots of this

Many crops grow well in the cool lands of northern Iraq, including sunflowers.

The Date Palm

Before the 1980s, when Iraq waged war against neighboring Iran, the country had more than thirty million date palms. Each year, the palms produced about one million tons of dates. For thousands of years, the date has played an important role in the economy and culture of Middle Eastern countries. The sweet, sticky fruit is an excellent source of vitamins and minerals and a good source of energy and fiber. But after years of war and neglect, the number of Iraq's date palms has fallen dramatically. The number of date processing factories has also dropped, from 150 before the 2003 invasion of Iraq to fewer than 20 today.

Recently, the Iraqi government has spent millions of dollars to boost the country's sagging date industry. Iraqi biologists have developed laboratory-grown date palms that are resistant to tree disease and bear fruit more quickly than traditional trees. New varieties of

dates are being introduced to improve the fruit's appeal both at home and in overseas markets. Date production is slowly increasing, and today Iraq is the fourth-leading date-producing country in the world.

plant are used to make a flavoring for candies and other sweet treats. In the marshlands, grasses and reeds grow in abundance, along with flowering plants such as pimpernels and geraniums.

The fertile soil and plentiful supply of rain make Iraq's north and northeast regions a haven for growing crops. Irrigation helps cultivate grains such as wheat and barley, which can otherwise only be grown in the valleys of the Tigris and Euphrates.

The northeast mountain region was once covered in large forests of oak trees. These have since been cut down for lumber. Pine, maple, willows, and hawthorns now make up the only forested areas found in the north.

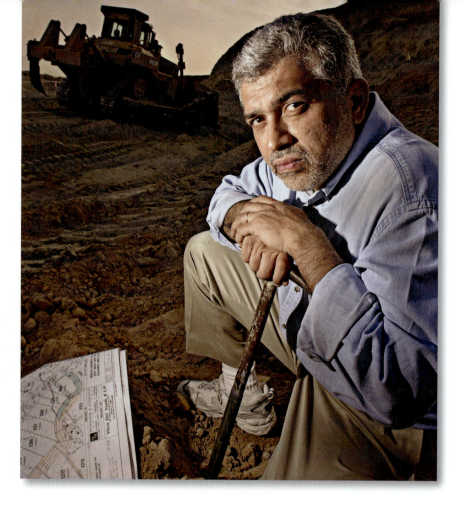

Azzam Alwash returned to Iraq in 2003 after living in the United States for more than two decades. In the years since, he has helped restore Iraq's southern marshes. In 2013, he was awarded the Goldman Environmental Prize, the world's leading prize for environmental activists.

Protecting, Restoring, and Preserving

Since the 1980s, Iraq has been involved in numerous destructive wars that have greatly harmed the environment. Bombings of industrial sites have released tons of toxic material into the environment. Further damage has been caused by government policies and neglect. Many delicate ecosystems and wildlife habitats have all but disappeared.

Iraqi engineer Azzam Alwash decided to take action to help his ailing country. After Saddam Hussein was ousted from power in 2003, Alwash established Nature Iraq, an environmental group. The organization's first project was to restore the southern marshlands. Since then, the group has worked to protect and restore other threatened habitats in Iraq. Alwash's goal is to establish a network of protected areas in the country, from the northern mountains through the southern plains and into the wetlands in the south.

Called Iraq's "wildlife guardian," Alwash continues his work even during his country's ongoing instability. Along with government officials and major industries, he is determined to solve Iraq's environmental problems. "Maybe it's not realistic right now," Alwash says, "but you have to dream big."

Only a small number of bears survive in Iraq. In 2017, several bears born in captivity were released into Halgurd Sakran National Park in northern Iraq in an attempt to increase the bear population.

CHAPTER 4

An Enduring Legacy

MESOPOTAMIA—THE ANCIENT LAND OF present-day Iraq—was the birthplace of civilization. It was there that the written history of human activity began. Its inspiring story is one of glory, conflict, change, and drama.

Enter the Sumerians

Around six thousand years ago, the Sumerians settled along the fertile lands of the Tigris and Euphrates Rivers in what is now modern Iraq. In the land called Sumer, people developed the basic tools of civilization, including advanced agricultural

Opposite: **Many powerful civilizations arose in Mesopotamia. The Akkadian civilization produced this bronze head, perhaps of King Sargon, which is considered one of the masterpieces of ancient art.**

The Village of Jarmo

In the 1940s, archaeologists made a stunning discovery in the foothills of the Zagros Mountains: the remains of what is believed to be one of the world's first village-farming communities. Located in Jarmo, east of Kirkuk, the nine-thousand-year-old site had been home to as many as 150 people. Covering an area of 4 acres (1.6 hectares), the village featured multiroomed houses built of mud brick. The inhabitants of Jarmo lived mainly on wheat, barley, and lentils. Their diet also included peas, pistachios, acorns, and snails. Bone was used to make spoons, buttons, and sewing needles.

Jarmo is one of the world's oldest sites where pottery has been found. Archaeologists have also discovered early figurines of animals and humans there, as well as tools made of obsidian, a black, glasslike rock. Because the closest source of the rock was located in present-day Turkey, historians believe the people of Jarmo engaged in long-distance trade with other cultures.

techniques such as irrigation. They invented the plow, the wheel, and an accurate calendar, and established the world's first formal school.

Sumer's most important development was the first known system of writing. Scribes etched symbols into soft clay tablets in a technique called cuneiform. Archaeologists have found hundreds of these tablets—the first written record of human civilization.

Such achievements allowed the Sumerians to largely abandon farming and to establish urban settlements. Mesopotamia blossomed into a major trading center with large, independent cities thriving along the Tigris and Euphrates.

About 2334 BCE, a man named Sargon from the city of Akkad to the north conquered Sumer and united Mesopotamia under his rule. Akkadian rule did not endure, however. In about 2000 BCE, the Babylonians conquered Mesopotamia and ruled for four hundred years. The city of Babylon became the capital of southern Mesopotamia. In 1792 BCE, the most famous Babylonian ruler, Hammurabi, came to power. During

The Ziggurat of Ur

The ancient Mesopotamians were the first to build structures known as ziggurats. A ziggurat is a tower built in steps. It has a flat top on which a temple was often placed.

The Great Ziggurat of Ur located in the Dhi Qar province in Iraq is one of Sumer's most spectacular remains. Built about four thousand years ago under King Ur-Nammu and his son, King Shulgi, the structure was dedicated to the Sumerian moon god Nanna. The massive pyramid measures 210 feet (64 m) long by 150 feet (46 m) wide. Originally, it was more than 100 feet (30 m) tall.

Unlike the limestone pyramids built in ancient Egypt, the Great Ziggurat of Ur was built with mud brick, a less durable material. Over the centuries, the structure crumbled into ruins. Nabonidus, a Babylonian king, had it restored in the sixth century BCE. Since then, the ziggurat has sometimes been damaged during wartime. For example, the Persian Gulf War of 1991 left it marked by bombs and bullets.

his reign, he created the first known set of laws. Called the Code of Hammurabi, it stated laws relating to personal property, the family, and other matters, as well as the punishments for breaking the laws.

As the centuries passed, the Babylonians came under frequent attack from outsiders. The most successful were the aggressive Assyrians from Nineveh, present-day Mosul, in northern Mesopotamia. In the ninth century, the Assyrians destroyed Babylon and seized control of Mesopotamia. In turn, the Chaldeans of southern Sumer took control of Babylon itself. In 612 BCE, the Chaldean king of Babylon, Nabopolassar, toppled the Assyrians. His son, King Nebuchadnezzar II, rebuilt

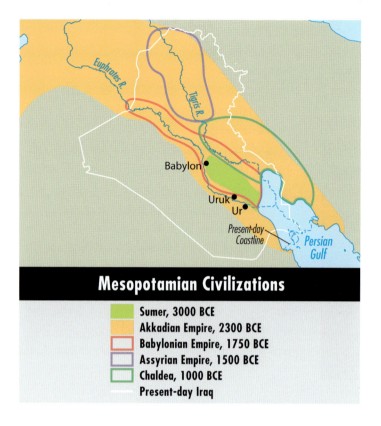

Mesopotamian Civilizations

- Sumer, 3000 BCE
- Akkadian Empire, 2300 BCE
- Babylonian Empire, 1750 BCE
- Assyrian Empire, 1500 BCE
- Chaldea, 1000 BCE
- Present-day Iraq

Babylon and reestablished control over most of Mesopotamia.

Nebuchadnezzar II was a great builder. He erected temples, palaces, and administrative buildings throughout the city. He may also have built the fabulous Hanging Gardens of Babylon, which is called one of the Seven Wonders of the Ancient World. The gardens featured lush vegetation growing in a series of terraces built into the outside walls of an 80-foot-high (24 m) structure.

After Nebuchadnezzar's death in about 561 BCE, Babylon's glory and power faded. In 539 BCE, Cyrus the Great of the Persian Empire, based in what is now Iran, conquered Mesopotamia. Over the next thousand years, control of the region frequently changed hands. At various times, the Greeks, Persian Parthians, Romans, and Persian Sassanids dominated the region.

The Muslim Empire

In the seventh century CE, the Prophet Muhammad founded the religion of Islam. By the time he died in 632, his followers, called Muslims, controlled the Arabian Peninsula. By 638, the Arab Muslims had conquered nearly all of Mesopotamia. The

No one has yet determined the exact location of the Hanging Gardens of Babylon, but many ancient authors discussed them. They were perhaps a series of irrigated terraces where many lush plants grew.

Muslim rulers were called caliphs. The fourth caliph, Ali, had his capital in Kufa, in what is now Iraq. The first great dynasty of Muslim rulers was the Umayyads dynasty. The Umayyads established their capital in Damascus, in present-day Syria. The people of Mesopotamia were unhappy under the Umayyads, and Kufa became a stronghold for opposition to the rule of the Umayyad dynasty. The Mesopotamians launched several rebellions to oust the Umayyads, but all attempts failed.

In 750, the Abbasids, who were a family that claimed to be descendants of Muhammad, overthrew the Umayyads and moved the capital of the empire to Baghdad. For four hundred

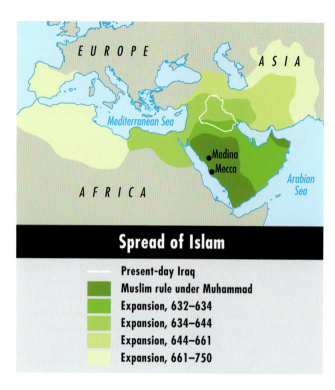

Spread of Islam

- Present-day Iraq
- Muslim rule under Muhammad
- Expansion, 632–634
- Expansion, 634–644
- Expansion, 644–661
- Expansion, 661–750

years, Baghdad was the hub of Islamic authority and the region's center of commerce and culture. Scholarship thrived in the great city, where people came to study and teach medicine, mathematics, chemistry, and more.

The Abbasids maintained control until 1258, when a Mongol army from Central Asia destroyed Baghdad and killed the last Abbasid caliph. In 1534, the Ottomans of Turkey seized Mesopotamia and made it part of the far-reaching Ottoman Empire.

The Ottomans appointed governors, judges, and other leaders. Some military was stationed in Iraq to help protect the Ottomans and their base in Turkey from more distant groups. By the 1600s, Ottoman authority had weakened, and Iraq was frequently the site of fighting between various tribes and groups. It remained part of the Ottoman Empire, however, for centuries.

European Influence

During World War I (1914–1918), the Ottoman Empire fought on the side of the Central powers, which also included Germany and Austria-Hungary. Their opposition was the Allied powers, which included France, Great Britain, Russia, the United States, and others. In 1917, British forces captured

The Father of Arabic Philosophy

Al-Kindi, who lived from about 801 to 873, was the most famous Muslim Arab philosopher of his day. Born in Basra, Al-Kindi studied in Baghdad where he translated Greek philosophical and scientific writings into Arabic. His work helped introduce these ancient writings to the Muslim world. He wrote many texts about philosophy, astronomy, mathematics, chemistry, and music. Al-Kindi's work emphasized that philosophy and religion dealt with the same subjects. Both, he believed, dealt with the knowledge and nature of God. Al-Kindi's work influenced scholars in the Muslim world and beyond, making possible the work of such significant thinkers as the Persian philosopher Avicenna.

Baghdad from the Turks. By the next year, they claimed most of Mesopotamia.

After the Allied victory, the League of Nations was formed to promote international cooperation. The organization confirmed British control of Iraq. In 1920, there was a military revolt against the British administration in southern and central Iraq. This uprising failed to end British control but prompted more powers to be transferred to the Iraqi state, which was formally founded in 1921. The British installed Faisal I as Iraq's king. Britain, however, continued to influence Iraq's military, political, and economic policies. Most Iraqis opposed any form of foreign influence. They carried out strikes and demonstrations to express their opposition to the British. Finally, in 1932, Iraq gained its complete independence and became a member in the League of Nations.

Oil was discovered in Iraq at Baba Gurgur near Kirkuk, in the northeast of the country, in 1927. By the 1950s, oil had become an important part of Iraq's economy.

Growing Pains

Uniting the new nation was a difficult challenge. Different religious groups, political movements, and ethnic groups competed for power and attention. King Faisal ruled until his death in 1933, at which time his son, Ghazi, took the throne. When Ghazi died in an automobile accident in 1939, his three-year-old son, Faisal II, became king.

Power in the monarchy fell to a cousin, Abd al-Ilah, until Faisal II became of age to rule. Al-Ilah was pro-British, as was Iraq's prime minister, Nuri al-Said. Most Iraqis continued to oppose Western influence. By the time World War II (1939–1945) began, a powerful movement of "Iraq for Iraqis" was brewing among the population—a sentiment shared by Iraqi armed forces.

In 1958, a military coup overthrew the monarchy. Twenty-three-year-old king Faisal II, Abd al-Ilah, and Nuri al-Said were murdered. One of the leaders of the coup, General Abd al-Karim Qasim, was named prime minister. The country was renamed the Republic of Iraq.

Five years later, the Baath Party, which adopted a radical Arab nationalist vision, staged a coup and killed Qasim. The party ruled briefly alongside President Abd al-Salem Arif. In 1966, Arif died in a plane crash, and two years later, the Baath Party came to power to stay.

Hussein Takes Power

Ahmad Hasan al-Bakr, a former prime minister, became president of Iraq, with Saddam Hussein as vice president. The Baath government improved Iraq's standard of living by upgrading education, health care, and agricultural production.

By this time, the Baath Party was dominated by leaders of Sunni origin. Islam is divided into two major sects, or groups, Sunni and Shi'a. About 60 percent of Iraqis are Shi'ites, but the people in power were Sunnis. Meanwhile, unrest was brewing among the Kurds, an ethnic minority living in north-

Abd al-Karim Qasim gave a press conference after leading the coup that overthrew the Iraqi monarchy in 1958. He became prime minister but was unable to bring stability to the country.

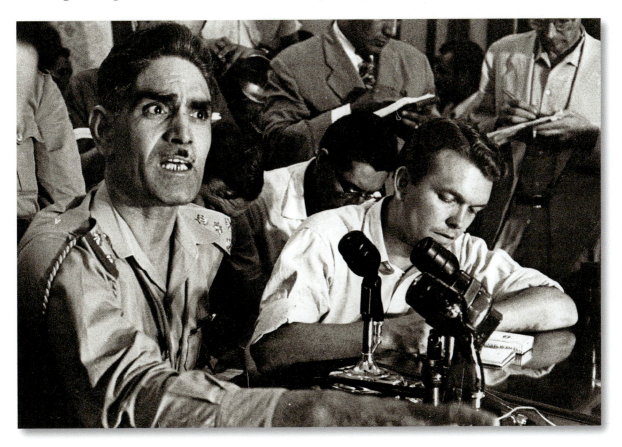

Saddam Hussein became president of Iraq in 1979 and remained in power for almost a quarter of a century.

ern Iraq and neighboring countries. Kurdish rebels staged frequent uprisings, battling the Iraqi army in an effort to gain greater independence.

In July 1979, Hussein forced al-Bakr to resign and he himself became president. The new head of state continued many of his predecessor's successful policies. But his leadership could also be brutal, as he cracked down hard on any perceived threats to his leadership.

In 1980, the Iraqi army invaded Shi'ite-dominated Iran. Hussein ordered the invasion because he feared that the new Islamic regime in Iran would encourage the Shi'ite majority in Iraq to rebel against him. Another goal of the invasion was to seize the oil-rich Iranian border province of Khuzestan.

The war was a dismal failure for Iraq. Eight years of fighting cost billions of dollars and took the lives of hundreds of thousands of Iraqi and Iranian soldiers and civilians. Ultimately, the border remained unchanged. Hussein did not secure Khuzestan. It was discovered that Hussein's forces had used chemical weapons not only against Iranian soldiers but also on Iraqi Kurds who were supported by Iran.

The Persian Gulf War

Two years after the Iran-Iraq war ended, Saddam Hussein started another costly war. In August 1990, Iraqi forces invaded Kuwait, an oil-rich country south of Iraq. The Iraqis easily overwhelmed Kuwait's forces. Hussein declared he was making Kuwait part of Iraq.

Many nations denounced Hussein's aggression. In January 1991, a coalition led by the United States began bombing raids to drive the Iraqis out of Kuwait. One month later, the coalition began ground operations. Hussein's army was quickly crushed, and within days, the Iraqis pulled out of the tiny nation.

After the invasion of Kuwait, the United Nations imposed economic sanctions on Iraq to prevent member nations from trading with Hussein. Almost every nation in the world belongs to the United Nations, an international organization dedicated to promoting peace around the world. The sanctions would have a devastating impact on the people of Iraq for years to come.

The Iraq War

On September 11, 2001, the extremist group al-Qaeda attacked the United States, killing thousands. None of the terrorists who carried out the attacks were Iraqi, but the U.S. government tried to link Saddam Hussein to the assault. President George W. Bush accused Iraq of sponsoring terrorism. He also claimed Iraq was stockpiling chemical, biological, and nuclear weaponry, known as weapons of mass destruction (WMD). Many experts, however, disputed the claims. Undeterred, the Bush administration argued that Hussein needed to be removed from power—for the safety of the Iraqi people and the world at large.

In March 2003, the United States and Great Britain invaded Iraq. Within a few weeks, troops entered Baghdad and captured Hussein. The Iraqi dictator was later tried and executed.

Any joy experienced by the Iraqi people was short-lived.

Saddam Hussein at his trial for crimes against humanity in 2006

Without a government, security broke down. Looting became widespread. Stores, hospitals, oil facilities, universities, and museums were destroyed. Priceless ancient artifacts were stolen. Iraqis soon began to link the U.S. presence in the country with the violence. Attacks on American troops became common.

Tens of thousands of insurgents turned to terrorism. The nation erupted into a civil war. Unemployment skyrocketed. Food shortages and lack of health care were rampant. Hundreds of thousands of Iraqis fled their homeland.

Meanwhile, a temporary Iraqi government was established in 2004. A new constitution was drafted and voted on in 2005. Soon thereafter, elections for the new government's legislature were held.

Violence continued, however, and the situation worsened every day. In 2007, President Bush ordered an increase in U.S. military forces in Iraq. The so-called surge helped reduce the

Iraqi soldiers inspect a building destroyed in fighting in Amarah, south of Baghdad. Iraq's long conflict has left many buildings as rubble.

An ISIS fighter mans a checkpoint along a highway.

violence. Many Iraqi refugees began returning to their homes. In December 2007, U.S. troops began withdrawing from Iraq. By the end of 2011, the last American forces left, bringing to a close the Iraq War—but not the violence that was spreading across Iraq.

The ISIS Threat

In June 2014, the terrorist group known as the Islamic State, or ISIS, launched an attack on the city of Mosul. ISIS is an offshoot of al-Qaeda. Iraqi government troops and police were overwhelmed, and the city fell within hours. In the midst of the bloodshed, thousands of Mosul residents fled the city.

The fighting spread and within two weeks ISIS controlled other important cities and towns nearby. In October 2016, having managed to retake most of those cities and towns, Iraqi government troops launched a joint operation with Kurdish forces to recapture Mosul. U.S. military advisers also participated in the action. The city was successfully recaptured in 2017.

The recent upheaval has been devastating for the people of Iraq. Today, there are about three million Iraqis who were forced from their homes, fleeing areas controlled by ISIS. They have sought refuge in Kurdistan, Baghdad, Najaf, and Karbala. After ISIS is defeated, there is much work that will need to be done. Cities have to be reconstructed, water systems repaired, schools built. But, given time, perhaps the Iraqi people will again live in a stable society.

In 2015, thousands of people fled their homes as ISIS gained control of parts of Al-Anbar province. More than three million Iraqis were forced from their homes by the conflict.

CHAPTER 5

The New Government

WITH THE FALL OF SADDAM HUSSEIN'S REGIME, Iraq began the task of creating a new government. In January 2005, Iraqi voters went to the polls to elect 275 representatives for the National Assembly of the Iraqi Transitional Government. A temporary body, its job was to draft a constitution for the nation. A second election would later be held to choose members of the permanent legislature.

Iraqi voters, however, were deeply divided.

Opposite: **An election official counts votes during the national election in 2014.**

The New Government **51**

پهرلهمانی کوردستان – عێراق

برلمان كوردستان – العراق

KURDISTAN PARLIAMENT - IRAQ

The Iraqi Kurdistan Parliament meets in Arbil, the capital of the Kurdistan region.

Sunnis, Shi'ites, and Kurds

Political power in Iraq has historically not been inclusive. Many parts of its diverse population have not had access to power. This has increased social tensions and the use of religious and ethnic categories as a way for each group to claim more power. The minority Sunni Arabs had dominated the Iraqi state since the birth of the nation in the 1920s. They feared losing power to the majority Shi'ite Arabs. In turn, the Shi'ites believed the time had finally arrived for them to assume a greater role in Iraqi politics. The Kurds, an ethnic minority, also wanted a strong voice in the new government. For years, the Kurds had struggled for self-rule and independence from Iraq. In 1992, the Kurds formed their own government, the Kurdistan Regional Government.

The Nation's Capital

With an estimated population of 7,216,000 in 2017, Baghdad, the capital of the Republic of Iraq, is the country's largest city. It is the second-largest city in the Arab world after Cairo, Egypt. It was founded in 762 by Abbasid caliphate Abu Jafar Al-Mansur, who decreed that the new city would be the capital of the Abbasid Empire. From the eighth to the thirteenth centuries, Baghdad reigned as the region's center of learning, culture, and commerce. The city was renowned for its superb libraries and schools, palaces and administrative buildings, and mosques. In 1258, Mongols from

eastern Asia captured Baghdad. The city fell into centuries of decline. After it became part of the Ottoman Empire in 1534, it once again began to prosper.

The Tigris River runs through Baghdad, dividing the city into two parts. Al-Karkh is the name of the section on the river's west bank, while the eastern section is known as Al-Rusafa. The city's main points of interest include the National Museum of Iraq, which displays art and artifacts from throughout Mesopotamia's rich history, the Baghdad Zoo, and the Al-Kadhimiya Mosque.

Until recently, Baghdad was a thriving metropolis of world-class cultural institutions. Since the Persian Gulf War and the Iraq War, however, the city has suffered significant damage to its buildings, and transportation, power, and sanitary systems. Even now, the threat of suicide bombings and large-scale attacks against the government and civilians is high.

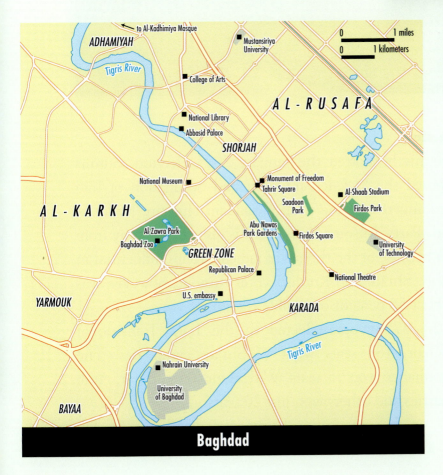

Baghdad

An Iraqi woman casts her ballot in the election in January 2005. In recent years, about 60 percent of eligible voters take part in Iraqi elections.

The Election

Most Sunnis boycotted the January 2005 election. Sunnis had opposed the U.S.-led invasion and occupation of Iraq and were angered by the trial of Saddam Hussein, leader of the Baath Party. In some cases, Sunnis also stayed away from the polls because of the threats of radical groups influential in their areas. Shi'ite and Kurdish voter turnout, however, was high. About 58 percent of eligible Iraqis cast votes.

Of the 275 people elected to the Iraqi Transitional Government, 180 seats went to Shi'ite candidates. The Kurdish alliance won 75 seats. With their low turnout, Arab Sunni parties and others won just 20 seats.

Work on the constitution began immediately. By the fall of 2005, a draft was ready to be voted on. A majority of Iraqis approved the constitution in October with a notable Sunni objection. In December, more Sunnis participated when Iraqis elected the first legislative body, the Council of Representatives. The Alliance of Shi'ite parties won most seats. By April 2006, the Council named Nuri al-Maliki, a Shi'ite, as the country's prime minister, and Jalal Talabani, a Kurd, as its president.

Maliki was named to a second term in 2010. In September 2014, Haider al-Abadi was named Iraq's prime minister. Muhammad Fuad Masum became president of Iraq in July 2014.

Muhammad Fuad Masum is the second consecutive ethnically Kurdish president of Iraq.

National Government of Iraq

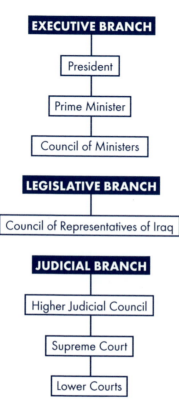

EXECUTIVE BRANCH

President

Prime Minister

Council of Ministers

LEGISLATIVE BRANCH

Council of Representatives of Iraq

JUDICIAL BRANCH

Higher Judicial Council

Supreme Court

Lower Courts

The Federal Government

According to the constitution of Iraq, the system of the nation's government is a democratic parliamentary republic. Islam is the state religion, and "no law that contradicts the established provisions of Islam may be established." The constitution establishes a government made up of three branches—the legislative, executive, and judicial.

The legislative, or lawmaking, branch is composed of two bodies, the Council of Representatives (COR) and the

Federation Council. As of 2017, the Federation Council had not yet been formed. Its responsibilities will be determined by the COR. The COR is made up of 328 elected representatives. Its main responsibilities are to make federal laws and appoint the president and members of federal courts. The COR also has the power to declare war and approve the national budget.

The executive branch consists of the president and the Council of Ministers. The president is head of state and is elected by a two-thirds majority of the COR for no more than two four-year terms. The president ratifies treaties and laws passed by the COR. A vice president assumes the duties of the president in case of his absence.

Members of Iraq's Council of Representatives raise their hands to vote. In 2017, 27 percent of the representatives were women.

The Iraqi Flag

Iraq's national flag has been redesigned many times over the years. In 1959, shortly after the military coup overthrew the monarchy of Faisal II, Iraq adopted a new flag. It consisted of three vertical stripes—black, white, and green. A red eight-pointed star with a yellow circle at its center appeared on the white stripe. The yellow circle represented the Kurdish minority. When the Baath Party came to power in 1963, the flag was changed to have three horizontal stripes of red, white, and black—the traditional colors of Arab people. Three five-pointed green stars were on the white stripe. In 1991, the phrase "God is great" written in Arabic was added in green to the white stripe.

After Saddam Hussein was driven from power in 2003, the Iraqi Governing Council designed a new national flag. The top part of the flag featured a light blue crescent on a horizontal white background. The bottom of the flag was three horizontal stripes of blue, yellow, and blue. Most Iraqis, who did not want to abandon the traditional Arab colors, rejected the flag.

In 2008, the Iraqi government adopted yet another flag: stripes of red, white, and black, with the white band containing "God is great" written in Kufic script, the oldest form of all Arabic scripts.

A judge in Mosul hears the details of a dispute between neighbors.

Haider al-Abadi

In September 2014, Haider al-Abadi became Iraq's prime minister. Al-Abadi was born in 1952 in Baghdad. He earned a bachelor's degree at the University of Technology in the capital city and earned a PhD in electrical engineering from the University of Manchester in England. In 1967, al-Abadi joined the Dawa Party, a Shi'ite political group and bitter foe of the Baath Party. While in England, al-Abadi became a leading Dawa figure and outspoken critic of the Hussein regime. The Baathists executed two of his brothers and would not allow him to return home. He remained in England until the 2003 invasion of Iraq.

That same year, he was named Iraq's minister of communications, a position he held until June 2004. The following year, he was elected to the Council of Representatives (COR), where he headed a committee to help rebuild Iraq's economy in the post-Hussein years. He was reelected in the 2010 elections and served as the chairman of COR's Finance Committee before becoming prime minister.

Since taking office, al-Abadi has made efforts to improve the Shi'ite-dominated government's relations with Sunnis and Kurds. Perhaps the greatest challenge the prime minister faces is the removal of ISIS insurgents from Iraq. Al-Abadi is confident that Iraqi forces and the limited number of U.S. advisers on the ground will get the job done.

The Council of Ministers is composed of the prime minister as head of government and his cabinet. The prime minister is the nation's highest executive and the commander in chief of Iraq's armed forces. The cabinet oversees important sectors of the country's activities, such as defense, finance, education, trade, and human rights.

The judicial branch is made up of numerous courts. The Supreme Court is the highest court in Iraq. It determines whether laws made by the COR are constitutional. Decisions of the Supreme Court are final. Lesser federal courts include the Central Criminal Court. The Higher Judicial Council oversees the work of the entire federal court system.

Local Government

Iraq is divided into nineteen provinces, which are further divided into districts. Al-Anbar in western Iraq is the largest province, measuring about 53,500 square miles (139,000 sq km), about the size of the U.S. state of New York. The province of Baghdad is the smallest, covering just the city and the surrounding metropolitan area.

A woman takes the oath of office as a provincial council member in Babil province, in central Iraq. Like U.S. state governments, Iraq's provincial governments make laws and provide services for their own regions. They have limited power, however, because they rely on the national government to finance their programs.

The National Anthem

"Mawtini" ("My Homeland") is the national anthem of Iraq. It was written by the Palestinian poet Ibrahim Tuqan and composed by the Lebanese composer Mohammed Flayfel. The anthem was adopted in 2004.

English translation

My homeland, my homeland,
Glory and beauty, sublimity, and splendor
Are in your hills, are in your hills.
Life and deliverance, pleasure and hope
Are in your air, are in your air.
Will I see you, will I see you?
Safely comforted and victoriously honored,
Safely comforted and victoriously honored.
Will I see you in your eminence?
Reaching to the stars, reaching to the stars,
My homeland, my homeland.

CHAPTER 6

Rebuilding for the Future

RAQ'S ECONOMY HAS BEEN SEVERELY DAMAGED BY three decades of war and violence. In recent years, the rise of the terrorist group ISIS within Iraq and a worldwide decline in oil prices has further harmed the nation's economy. The violence has scared off international investors, significantly reducing foreign investment.

Iraq's unemployment rate is high, hovering at roughly 17 percent in 2017—a drop from a high of more than 25 percent in early 2015. Among young people ages seventeen to twenty-five, unemployment runs about 60 percent.

Opposite: **A construction worker on the site of a new water treatment plant near Baghdad. Less than 20 percent of Iraqis work in industry such as construction or manufacturing.**

Money Facts

The dinar is the basic unit of Iraqi currency. In 2017, 1,169 dinars equaled US$1. In 2003 and 2004, Iraq issued new banknotes, or paper money, and new dinar coins. The coins come in values of 23, 50, and 100 dinars. The bills come in eight denominations of dinars: 50, 250, 500, 1,000, 5,000, 10,000, 25,000, and 50,000. The illustrations on each bill relate to an important aspect of Iraqi life. For example, the 5,000-dinar note has an image of the Geli Ali Beg waterfall in Iraqi Kurdistan on the front and the ancient Abbasid palace of Ukhaidir on the back.

The 50,000-dinar banknote was introduced in November 2015. An Assyrian jar, a waterwheel on the Euphrates, palm trees, and the Geli Ali Beg waterfall appear on the front. The back has an outline map of Iraq showing the Tigris and Euphrates Rivers, and images of the Great Mosque of Samarra, a fisherman poling a raft through marshes, and animals.

The nation continued to experience significant woes even after the lifting of economic sanctions following the fall of Saddam Hussein. The 2003 invasion damaged or destroyed much of the country's infrastructure. Buildings, bridges, roads, and pipelines, and water supply, telecommunications, electrical, and sewage systems desperately require upgrading. The weak economy has made repair and recovery a difficult challenge for the nation.

The Oil Industry

Since the 1930s, the oil industry has been the backbone of the Iraqi economy. Today, oil accounts for about 90 percent of government revenue. Iraq's proven oil reserves amount to more than 150 billion barrels. Most of the oil reserves are located in the northern and eastern parts of Iraq.

Since 2010, oil production has steadily been on the rise. In 2009, Iraq produced about 2.4 million barrels of oil a day. By early 2017, production reached 4.6 million barrels daily, making Iraq one of the world's leading oil producers. Iraq uses about 20 percent of the oil it produces and exports about 80 percent, with more than half going to India and China. The United States receives about 8 percent of Iraq's oil exports. Iraq's natural gas reserves are also vast.

In 2009, Iraq's Ministry of Oil awarded service contracts to giant international oil companies, including Shell, BP, ExxonMobil, and China National Petroleum Corporation. The twenty-year agreements will provide Iraq with much-needed billions of dollars to bolster the nation's shaky economy.

Iraq has the fifth-largest oil reserves of any country. Although frequent war and conflict have hampered Iraq's ability to fully exploit its oil reserves, oil still accounts for 98 percent of the nation's exports.

What Iraq Grows, Makes, and Mines

AGRICULTURE	
Wheat (2013)	4,178,379 metric tons
Barley (2013)	1,003,198 metric tons
Sheep (2014)	8,200,000 animals

MANUFACTURING (VALUE OF EXPORTS, 2015)	
Chemical products	$92,800,000
Machines	$15,300,000

MINING (2016)	
Oil (2016)	4,647,800 barrels per day
Natural gas (2016)	10,416,400,000 cubic meters
Limestone (2013)	5,500,000 metric tons

Agriculture

War and economic sanctions have devastated agriculture in Iraq, where farming began thousands of years ago. In the 1970s, nearly 50 percent of the Iraqi labor force worked in agriculture. Today, about 20 percent of Iraqis engage in farming. Agricultural land accounts for about 18 percent of the land in Iraq, but only 8 percent of it is suitable for farming. Pasture makes up most of Iraq's agricultural land.

A wide range of crops is grown in the rain-fed northeast, including wheat, barley, chickpeas, olives, sunflowers, tobacco, and lentils. Southern Iraq depends on irrigation to produce crops such as grains, rice, cotton, corn, melons, green beans, onions, and eggplants. Dozens of varieties of date palms

are grown in the southern and central parts of the country.

In well-watered rural areas, Iraqis raise sheep, goats, cattle, and water buffalo for meat, milk, and hides. The numbers of sheep and goats in Iraq have sharply declined in the last thirty years. During that time, the human population has nearly doubled. To make up for the lack of these foodstuffs, Iraq imports most of the food it consumes, including large quantities of meat, poultry, grains, and dairy products.

A boy sits on one of his family's water buffaloes in a river in Baghdad. Many Iraqis in the marshlands keep buffaloes, which produce rich milk.

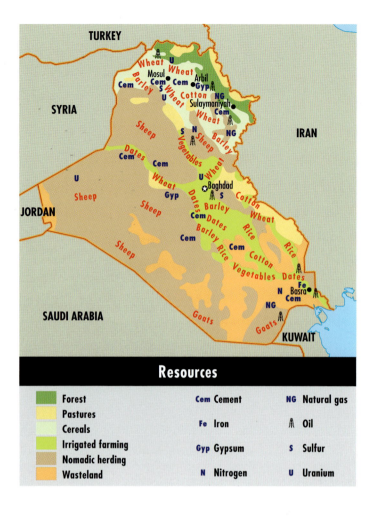

Resources

Forest	**Cem** Cement	**NG** Natural gas
Pastures		
Cereals	**Fe** Iron	Oil
Irrigated farming		
Nomadic herding	**Gyp** Gypsum	**S** Sulfur
Wasteland	**N** Nitrogen	**U** Uranium

Manufacturing

Aside from the oil industry, manufacturing in Iraq is largely undeveloped. Manufactured goods include textiles, leather, chemicals, foods and beverages, and construction materials such as cement and bricks. Baghdad, Basra, and the Kirkuk-Arbil region are the nation's leading manufacturing centers.

Services

About 60 percent of working Iraqis are employed in service industries. Most of them work for the government in the fields of education, health care, or security. Many others work in retail stores or in banking. Economic sanctions severely hurt Baghdad's once-thriving service industries. Today, most of the city's shops are small family-owned businesses.

Forestry and Fishing

Centuries of deforestation have reduced the amount of forested land in Iraq to less than 2 percent. Nearly all of the country's natural forests are in the mountainous northeast region. Iraq does not export any of the timber it produces.

A man sells tomatoes at a busy market in northern Iraq.

Instead, Iraqis use the forests mainly for construction, firewood, and charcoal. Wood for large construction projects and furniture manufacturing must be imported. The government has launched several small-scale reforestation projects to increase the supply of timber.

Despite an abundance of rivers, Iraq's fishing industry is small. Most fish is consumed locally, and is not an important export item for Iraq. Carp, mullet, catfish, and shad are pulled from Iraq's inland waterways. Some fishing is done in the Persian Gulf. Fish farms produce large quantities of carp.

Transportation

Iraq's transportation system is a combination of the ancient and the modern. Camels, donkeys, and horses are still used in some rural areas, such as the mountains and deserts. High-quality highways and railways service the major regions of the country.

Iraq has about 37,000 miles (60,000 km) of paved roadways. Many of the roads and bridges were destroyed in recent wars but were repaired in subsequent years. Four-lane highways link Iraq's largest cities and provide access to neighboring countries. Most Iraqis are unable to afford cars, but for those who can, gasoline is inexpensive: about US$0.15 a gallon in 2017.

The Iraqi Republic Railways Company (IRR) operates the national railroad system. The system mainly handles com-

Large streets run through the center of Sulaymaniyah, in northeastern Iraq.

mercial traffic and shipping. Major lines in the north run from Baghdad to Kirkuk and Arbil, and from Baghdad to Mosul and Turkey. To the south, a line connects Baghdad with Basra and Umm Qasr, and a line extending eastward links the interior of Iraq with Syria.

Almost entirely landlocked, all of Iraq's port facilities are located on the lower Shatt al-Arab waterway. The port of Basra, close to many of Iraq's large oil and gas fields, is the nation's largest.

Iraq has about one hundred airports, of which about seventy have paved runways. The Baghdad International Airport is the nation's largest, handling about 7.5 million passengers a year. It is the home base for Iraq's national airline, Iraqi Airways. From 1990 to 2014, the airline was sometimes grounded by war and economic sanctions.

CHAPTER 7

Arabs and Kurds

RAQ'S POPULATION OF 39 MILLION PEOPLE INCLUDES several different ethnic groups. Most Iraqis—about 80 percent of the population—are Arabs. Kurds, the largest minority group, make up about 15 percent. Small numbers of Turkmen, Assyrians, Persians, and Armenians also live in Iraq.

Growing Cities

Iraq's average population density is about 220 people per square mile (85 per sq km). The population density varies greatly across the nation, however. On average, fewer than three people per square mile live in the west and the deserts in the south. More than 2,000 people per square mile

Population of Major Cities (2017 est.)	
Baghdad	7,216,000
Basra	2,600,000
Mosul	1,739,800
Arbil	932,800
Sulaymaniyah	723,170

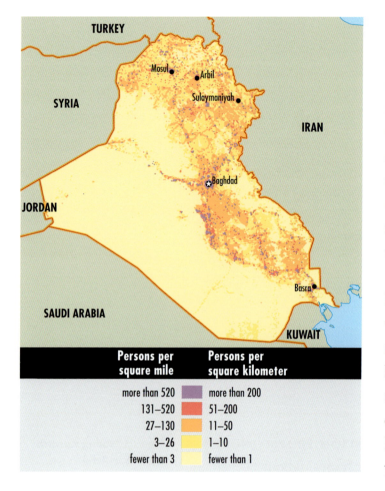

Persons per square mile		Persons per square kilometer
more than 520		more than 200
131–520		51–200
27–130		11–50
3–26		1–10
fewer than 3		fewer than 1

(770 per sq km), however, live in large cities such as Baghdad and Basra. About 70 percent of the country's population lives in such urban regions. Each year, the number of city dwellers increases, as people move away from rural areas to find work in the larger urban areas.

Iraq has one of the highest birth rates in the Arab world, with women having an average of about four children. The high birth rate strains a nation already plagued by high levels of poverty and unemployment. Iraq's population is relatively young, with more than 50 percent under the age of fifteen.

Arabs

Arabs are the largest ethnic group in the Middle East and northern Africa, comprising a total population of about 200 million people. Roughly 30 million Arabs live in Iraq. An Arab is anyone who speaks Arabic as their first language. Arabs share a culture and history. Most Arabs are Muslim, but some are Christian, Jewish, or belong to smaller religious minorities. Others do not identify with any religious group.

Iraq's Ethnic Groups

Arab	75% to 80%
Kurdish	15% to 20%
Other (Turkmen, Assyrian, etc.)	5%

Iraqi Bedouin are nomadic Arabs who have traditionally traveled between the country's urban centers and the large expanses of western desert. In recent years, many Bedouin have abandoned their nomadic lifestyle and set up farming villages close to cities. Large numbers of Bedouin have settled in the Babil and Wasit provinces located south and southeast of Baghdad, respectively.

Kurds

The Kurds have lived in the foothills and mountains of northern Iraq for as many as four thousand years. The region is known as Iraqi Kurdistan. The Iraqi Kurds belong to a larger Kurdish population that extends into Turkey, Iran, and Syria. The Kurds are believed to be the world's largest ethnic group without its own state. Most Kurds are Sunni Muslim, although several small groups belong to the Shi'a

A Bedouin woman prepares dough for bread in a tent in southern Iraq. Hundreds of thousands of Bedouin live in Iraq.

Kurdish children take part in a celebration in the northern Iraqi town of Aqrah. Kurds follow a variety of religious practices. In Iraq, 98 percent of Kurds are Sunni Muslim, while in neighboring Iran, about half the Kurds are Sunni, and half are Shi'ite.

sect and other religious minorities. Some Kurds do not tend to identify with any religious group.

The Kurds were originally nomads, tending goats and sheep as they moved from place to place. After World War I (1914–1918), however, their ancestral homelands were given to other nations to govern. No longer free to herd where they desired, the Kurds moved to cities or settled down to farm.

The Kurds have historically maintained stronger ties to their own groups and culture than to the local or national governments in the lands where they have lived. For decades, they have battled the central government—including Saddam Hussein's government in Baghdad—to establish their own self-government in Kurdistan. In the late 1980s and early 1990s, Hussein struck back, attacking Kurdish settlements with chemical weapons and all-out military assaults. In 2003, the militia formed by Iraqi Kurds—the *peshmerga*—fought alongside U.S.-led coalition forces during the invasion of Iraq. In recent years, the peshmerga has teamed up with Iraqi and U.S. forces in the fight against ISIS. Despite this cooperation, disputes between

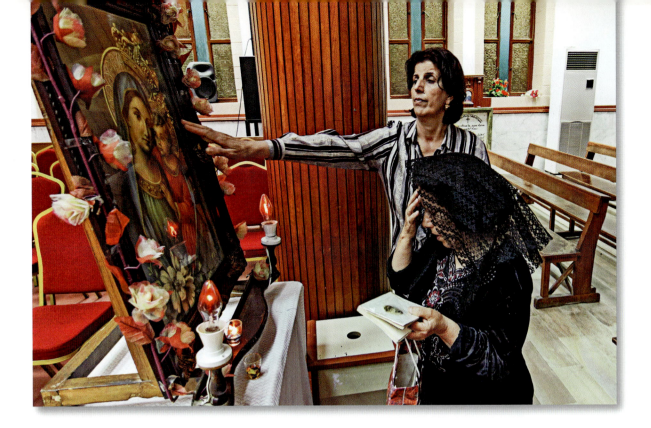

the Kurds and the Iraqi national government over territory and resources have not been resolved.

Other Groups

Apart from the Kurds, a small percentage of Iraq's population is composed of other minority groups. The Turkmen are the third-largest ethnic group in Iraq, accounting for about 3 percent of the country's total population. They live in villages in the northeast near Kirkuk, Mosul, and Arbil. The Turkmen are descendants of Mongol invaders from Central Asia. They speak a dialect of the Turkish language. Most Turkmen are Sunni Muslim.

The Assyrians trace their roots to the ancient Mesopotamians. They speak a form of Aramaic that has existed in Iraq for more

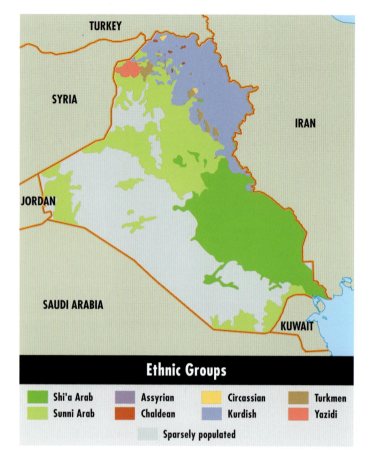

Ethnic Groups

🟩 Shi'a Arab	🟪 Assyrian	🟨 Circassian	🟫 Turkmen
🟩 Sunni Arab	🟥 Chaldean	🟦 Kurdish	🟥 Yazidi
	Sparsely populated	

than 3,200 years. Assyrians live mainly in the northeast and are mostly Christian.

The Armenians, another Christian minority, have lived in Iraq since late Babylonian times. Large numbers of Armenians came to Iraq in the early seventeenth and early twentieth centuries when Ottoman Turks forced them out of eastern Turkey. Iraqi Armenians live mainly in Baghdad and the northern cities of Mosul, Kirkuk, and Dohuk.

The Ajam people of Iraq are of Persian Iranian descent. They belong to the Shi'a sect of Islam. In the 1970s and early 1980s, Saddam Hussein deported hundreds of thousands of Iraqi Persians. Many fled to Iran, as they did later during the Iran-Iraq War (1980–1988). The Ajam live mainly near the Shi'ite holy cities of Najaf, Karbala, and Samarra.

The Languages of Iraq

Iraq has two official languages: Arabic and Kurdish. Arabic is spoken by about 80 percent of the population, while Kurdish is spoken by about 15 percent.

Arabic has several different common dialects in Iraq. The main forms are Mesopotamian, spoken throughout most of Iraq, and North Mesopotamian, used in the far northern parts of the country.

Kurdish has two dialects in Iraq. Sorani, or the Central dialect, is most common in Arbil, Kirkuk, and Sulaymaniyah. Kurmanji, or the Northern dialect, is spoken farther north, around Dohuk and Mosul.

Iraq's minority populations speak a variety of other languages. Turkmen speak Azeri Turkish. Persian is heard in areas along the Iraq-Iran border. Armenian is spoken in Baghdad, while different dialects of Aramaic are used in Mosul, Basra, and southeastern Iraqi Kurdistan.

The Kurdish language is written using the Arabic alphabet.

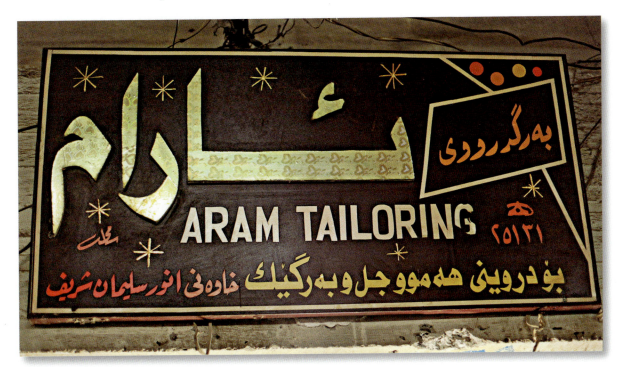

Common Arabic Words and Phrases

Sa-bah al-khair	good morning
As-sa-lam a-lay-kum	hello (peace be upon you)
Ma sa-la-ma	good-bye (with peace)
Na'am	yes
La	no
Shu-kran	thank you
Mini fad-lak	please (to a man)
Mini fad-lik	please (to a woman)
Kaif-hal-ak?	How are you?
Sa-deeq	friend
Kum?	How much?
Is-mi . . .	My name is . . .

Syrian Refugees

Since the beginning of Syria's civil war in 2011, more than five million Syrians have fled their country. More than 250,000 Syrian refugees have sought safety in Iraq. The majority of them are Kurds, who came from northeastern Syrian provinces. An estimated 97 percent of all Syrian refugees in Iraq live in Kurdistan. More than 40 percent of the refugees are children.

The Kurdistan Regional Government (KRG) has built camps to house the Syrians and has provided about $70 million in relief monies. The KRG is working closely with the United Nations (UN) and other partners to provide food, shelter, and health care to the displaced Syrians.

Life is difficult for the Syrians living in the refugee camps, but far safer than conditions back home. In some of the camps, refugees have started their own small businesses, such as barbershops and restaurants. The KRG has also allowed many of the refugees to travel and work outside the camps. "This allows the refugees possible ways to regain self-reliance . . . to earn money and bring it back to their families," says Liene Veide of the United Nations Refugee Agency.

Syrian children walk to school at a refugee camp in northern Iraq. As the conflict has continued, the camps have come to resemble new cities.

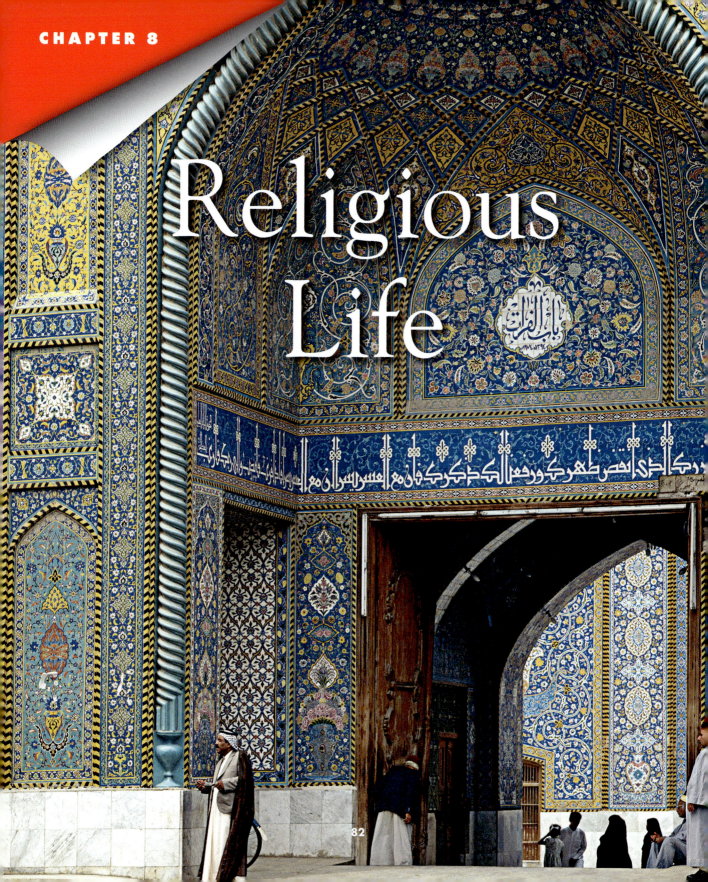

CHAPTER 8

Religious Life

ISLAM IS THE OFFICIAL RELIGION OF THE REPUBLIC of Iraq. About 99 percent of the Iraqi population is Muslim. The other 1 percent practices a number of other religions, including Christianity, Mandaeism, Yazidism, Hinduism, Buddhism, and folk religion. Though Islam dominates Iraq's religious culture, the nation's constitution "guarantees the full religious rights of all individuals to freedom of religious belief and practice."

Opposite: **Many mosques in Iraq are covered with ornate tile work.**

Some Muslims use prayer beads to keep track of the number of times they've recited a certain phrase. For some people, it is the practice to repeat phrases praising God ninety-nine times.

The Birth of Islam

According to tradition, an Arab merchant named Muhammad founded Islam in the seventh century. Muhammad was born around 570 in the city of Mecca, in present-day Saudi Arabia. At age forty, while meditating alone in a cave in Mecca, the angel Gabriel is said to have appeared to him many times. During these visitations, Gabriel is believed to have delivered divine messages from God—"Allah" in Arabic—to Muhammad.

Muhammad began to spread the sacred message to his Arab neighbors. He urged them to abandon their religions of many gods, and to turn away from Judaism and Christianity. Muhammad's message began to attract many followers. They compiled the messages Muhammad had received into the Qur'an, the holy book of Islam. (The word *Islam* means "submission to God" in Arabic.) As the new religion spread, Muhammad faced strong opposition from the residents of Mecca, who worshipped many gods. In 622, Muhammad and his followers left Mecca and settled in the city of Medina. This migration is called the *Hijra*.

Muhammad continued to attract newcomers to Islam by the tens of thousands. At the time of his death in 632, nearly the entire Arab population in the Arabian Peninsula had converted to Islam.

The Five Pillars of Islam

Worldwide, more than 1.6 billion people—23 percent of earth's total population—are Muslim. Islam is the world's

Muslims pray five times a day: at dawn, midday, late afternoon, sunset, and night. The call to prayer, indicating when it is time to pray, is announced from the top of a tall tower called a minaret, which is part of a mosque.

second-largest religion, after Christianity, and is the fastest-growing religion in the world. Islam is based on a set of guiding principles called the Five Pillars of Islam, which Muslims around the world are required to follow.

The first pillar, the *shahadah*, is the most basic expression of Islamic beliefs. Muslims are required to proclaim their faith, saying, "There is no god but God and Muhammad is the messenger of God." The second pillar, *salah*, is the call to daily prayers. Muslims are required to pray five times a day. They can pray anywhere, but must always pray toward Mecca. *Zakat*, the third pillar, is the command to give charity to the poor and needy. The fourth pillar, *saum*, is the fasting during the holy month of Ramadan, the ninth month in the Islamic calendar. Each day during the month, Muslims are expected to fast from dawn to dusk. The fifth and final pillar is the *hajj*, which obliges Muslims to make the pilgrimage to the holy city of Mecca at least once in their lives.

Each day during Ramadan, Muslims break their fast after sunset with a meal called iftar. In some places, large communal iftars are held.

To Mecca

The *hajj* is the fifth of the basic Muslim practices known as the Five Pillars of Islam. This practice instructs all Muslims to make a pilgrimage, or hajj, to Mecca at least once in their lifetime. The hajj takes place from the eighth to twelfth of Dhu al-Hijjah, the twelfth and final month of the Islamic calendar. The hajj is the world's largest annual gathering. Each year, more than three million Muslim pilgrims journey to Mecca from around the world—by airplane, automobile, bus, train, boat, and by foot or on camel.

Before entering Mecca, pilgrims put on the *ihram*, a white, two-piece garment for men and a white gown and scarf for women. Once in the holy city, they walk around the shrine called the Kaaba, a square building draped in a black cloth, seven times. This ritual is called *tawaf*. The sacred shrine is located in the Great Mosque, an enormous courtyard with prayer areas. Later that day, the pilgrims walk or run seven times between the hills of Safa and Marwah located near the Kaaba. They spend the night in prayer in the city of Mina.

The next day, the pilgrims gather at the Mount of Mercy at Arafat, a plain about 12 miles (20 km) east of Mecca. They pray for hours asking God's forgiveness for their sins. That night on the journey back to Mecca, they collect pebbles at the town of Muzdalifah, where they spend the night. The following morning, they return to Mina and perform a symbolic "stoning of the devil" by throwing the pebbles at a wall. Then they continue on to Mecca, where they circle the Kaaba and pass once more between the hills of Safa and Marwah.

The pilgrims remain in Mecca for two or three nights and then return to Mina to stone the devil a second time. In the final act of the hajj, the pilgrims go back to Mecca for a final circling of the Kaaba.

During the hajj, each pilgrim is required to slaughter and sacrifice an animal, usually a sheep, goat, or camel. Today most pilgrims buy a "sacrifice voucher," in which an animal is slaughtered in the name of God, without the pilgrim being present. Meat from the animals is given to the poor and needy around the world.

This Qur'an was created in the 1300s in Baghdad.

Holy Writings

The Qur'an is a collection of all the revelations that God is said to have sent to Muhammad through the angel Gabriel. Soon after Muhammad died, his followers compiled the messages into a single book. The Qur'an does not contain the thoughts or sayings of the Prophet Muhammad. It is believed the words in the Qur'an are the words of God himself.

The Qur'an is broken into 114 chapters called *surahs*. Each chapter except one begins with the phrase, "In the name of Allah the most merciful and the most kind." Like the Old Testament in the Bible, the Qur'an tells the story of the creation of the first humans, Adam and Eve. It also describes the Day of Judgment and the lives of past prophets such as Noah, Abraham, and Moses. God's grace and goodness toward humanity is explained, as is God's ability to punish those who do evil.

The Qur'an also serves as a guidebook for Muslim daily life. Among its more than 77,000 words are guidelines regarding law, food, clothing, charity, education, the role of women, and business and community organization.

The *hadith* is another important body of Islamic religious writings. The word *hadith* means "news" or "story" in the Arabic language. This body of work is a collection of narrations about the life of Muhammad. Like a biography, it reports his words, actions, and teachings. The hadith expands on the Qur'an's authority regarding religious law and moral guidance. It reveals more about social and personal matters, such as forgiveness, respect, and health. Shi'a and Sunni traditions regarding the hadith slightly differ. Nevertheless, all Muslims view the Qur'an and the hadith together as the basis for the Islamic legal system and the code of Muslim behavior.

Sunnis and Shi'ites

Not all Iraqis belong to the same branch of Islam. The religion is divided into two large sects, Sunni and Shi'a. Over the centuries, relations between the two groups have shaped the history of Iraq. The division of Islam arose after the death of the Prophet Muhammad. Different groups disagreed about who should succeed Muhammad as the leader, or caliph, of all Muslims. The Sunnis believed the caliph should be chosen from a group of elite Muslims. The Shi'ites held that the

Religion in Iraq	
Muslims	99%
Shi'ites	55–60%
Sunnis	40%
Others (including Christians, Yazidis, Mandaeans, Baha'is, Zoroastrians, Hindus, Buddhists, Jews, and more)	1%

caliph had to be a direct descendant of the prophet. They insisted Muhammad had designated his son-in-law Ali Ibn Abi Talib as his successor, called an imam. In turn, Ali picked his successor.

The Shi'ites believed their religious leaders had the divine right to lead. For this reason, they did not recognize the authority of Sunni caliphs. The Sunnis recognized the authority of all caliphs who ruled after Muhammad and did not limit the right to lead the Muslim community to the prophet's descendants.

Most of the world's Muslims are Sunni. In Iraq, however,

Shi'ites visit the shrine of al-Husayn ibn Ali in Karbala. Husayn, a grandson of Muhammad and the third Shi'ite leader, was killed in Karbala in a conflict over Muslim leadership.

A Sacred Shrine

For Shi'a Muslims, the Ali Ibn Abi Talib Shrine in Najaf, also known as the Mosque of Ali, is the holiest site in

Iraq. The mosque contains the tomb of Imam Ali Ibn Abi Talib, the son-in-law and cousin of Muhammad. Ali was regarded as the prophet's true successor to lead the Muslim people. In 661, Ali was assassinated and buried at Najaf. The mosque was first built in 977 over Ali's tomb. It was rebuilt two more times, once in 1086 and again shortly after 1500.

According to Shi'a tradition, the biblical figures Abraham and his son, Isaac, once visited the ancient village of Najaf. Shi'ites also believe the remains of Adam and Eve are buried next to Ali in the mosque. Each year, more than eight million Shi'ite pilgrims visit the sacred shrine, and the shrine of Ali's son, Husayn, who was killed along with his family members in the city of Karbala by the Umayyad army.

Shi'ites make up about 55 to 60 percent of Muslims, while Sunnis comprise about 40 percent. Historically, the two groups traded and intermarried. However, government leaders sometimes favored one group over another. Even though Saddam Hussein's regime was not religious, for many decades it supported loyal groups who happened to be Sunnis, so as a whole, before 2003 Sunnis in Iraq held more political power than Shi'ites. They enjoyed better economic and educational opportunities, and held more prestigious positions in the government and in the military.

The Shi'ites deeply resented these inequalities. After Saddam Hussein's ouster from power, the Shi'ites gained control of the new Iraqi government. Violence between militias and armed groups belonging to the two groups escalated in 2006 and 2007,

Sunni Muslims pray at a mosque in Baghdad.

and resumed again in 2014 when ISIS, an extremist group, controlled most of the Sunni majority cities.

Other Religions

About 1 percent of Iraqis practice a religion other than Islam. In the past, however, many religions peacefully coexisted in this region. Christianity arrived in Iraq in the first century CE. In the middle of the twentieth century, Christians still comprised about 10 percent of Iraq's population. But more recent political developments have reduced the religious diversity of Iraq. For example, after the U.S.-led invasion in 2003 ousted Hussein, there was little state authority or security. Violence

Ali al-Sistani

Ali al-Sistani, commonly known as Grand Ayatollah, is Shi'a Islam's leading religious authority. The term *ayatollah* is a title given to Shi'a clerics, or top-ranking religious figures. Al-Sistani played a critical role in the creation of the new Iraqi government after Saddam Hussein was ousted from power. He continues to be a strong voice calling for political and social reform in Iraq.

Born in 1930 in Mashhad, Iran, al-Sistani is the son of Sayyid Muhammad Baqir, a religious scholar. He began studying religion at the age of five, first in his hometown and then later in Qom, Iran. In 1952, he moved to Iraq to study in Najaf, where he rose through the ranks to become a senior cleric within the Shi'a religious community. In the mid-1990s, he became the leader of Najaf's religious schools and developed a large following of students in Iraq and neighboring Arab countries.

After the fall of Hussein, American and Iraqi officials planned to appoint several committees that would slowly create the first national legislature. Al-Sistani disagreed with this plan and called for an immediate election to choose a government for Iraq. Thousands of his supporters staged demonstrations and protests demanding elections. In the end, the officials agreed, and elections were held in December 2005.

In 2014, al-Sistani called on Iraqis to volunteer in the fight against ISIS. As a result, the Popular Mobilization Forces (PMF) was formed. Now in his late eighties, experts are uncertain what role al-Sistani's millions of supporters will play in the future of Iraqi politics once he dies.

Christians attend an Easter service at a church near Mosul. The northern part of Iraq has the largest number of Christians.

grew, and religious extremist groups persecuted the Christian population of Iraq. Seeking safety, many Iraqi Christians fled their country into neighboring Syria, Lebanon, and Jordan.

The Yazidis practice a religion that combines aspects of Judaism, Christianity, Islam, and Zoroastrianism, a seventh-century BCE belief system that originated in Iran. Yazidis believe in one god who created the world with the assistance of seven angels and placed it in their care. The Yazidis live in Iraqi Kurdistan, where the village of Lalish contains the holiest temple in the Yazidi faith.

The Mandaeans have inhabited Iraq since about the third century CE. They are followers of John the Baptist, a prophet revered by Muslims and Christians. They also follow figures from the Old Testament, though they reject other major biblical figures, including Abraham, Moses, and Jesus. Since the 2003 invasion, Mandaeans, like other minority groups, have faced oppression and violence. By 2007, tens of thousands of Iraqi Mandaeans were refugees living in Syria and Jordan.

On Yazidi New Year, which falls in April, people light oil lamps and candles to commemorate the arrival of light into the world.

CHAPTER 9

Rich Traditions

MESOPOTAMIA, THE LAND THAT IS NOW IRAQ, is sometimes called the Cradle of Civilization. Ancient Mesopotamian artisans produced spectacular works of art in ceramic, stone, gold and silver, gemstones, shells, and mosaics. Builders created stunning, monumental architecture, such as the Ziggurat of Ur, that stands to this day.

The spread of Islam throughout the Arabian Peninsula brought with it new, creative forms of art. Colorful, ornate geometric and floral designs adorned luxurious carpets, glass objects, carved ivories, glazed ceramics, delicately handwoven silks, and more. The land that introduced cuneiform, the world's first writing, was also home to Arabic calligraphy, a handwriting style that has been called "the Islamic art of

Opposite: **Beautiful calligraphy and floral designs decorate the Jalil Khayat mosque in Arbil.**

Abdul Qadir al-Rassam painted this scene of the Tigris River in 1920.

arts." Using the creative and versatile script, scribes recorded the Qur'an and other religious texts on parchment and paper. Craftspeople incorporated calligraphy into ceramics, wood, textiles, glass, and metal, creating works of art that continue to awe and inspire even in modern times.

Art

Many modern painters have made a name for themselves in Iraq. The first well-known painter in modern Iraq, Abdul Qadir al-Rassam studied art in Istanbul, Turkey, in the early twentieth century. He was an influential landscape and portrait painter, creating notable works in a realistic style, mainly in oils.

Musaddak Jameel Al-Habeeb is a modern calligrapher who uses bold, striking colors, unlike traditional Arabic calligraphy, which primarily uses black inks.

Art and Politics

Iraqi artist Dia Azzawi is a pioneer of modern Arab art. His unique drawings, sculptures, and artist's books (visual depictions of Arab poems) are displayed in the Middle East and in Western museums. His creations are politically charged and controversial.

Azzawi was born in 1939 in Baghdad. By day he studied archaeology at the College of Arts in the capital city. At night he studied painting at the Institute of Fine Arts. In his early works, he used Arab stories from ancient Mesopotamia to comment on the political unrest in Iraq during the 1960s.

In 1963, Azzawi was arrested by the Baath Party on suspicion of being a communist. He served two months in prison. Between 1966 and 1973, he reluctantly served in the Iraqi army, where he fought Kurdish rebels. "It felt," he said, "like I was fighting friends."

After he left military service, Azzawi began working on a series of paintings called *Human States*, in which he tried to bring attention to the hardships of the Kurds in northern Iraq. With the Baath Party growing more powerful, Azzawi left Iraq and moved to London, where he still lives today.

The 2003 invasion of Iraq motivated Azzawi to create his most political commentaries in art. He wished to illustrate the effect of the invasion on Iraq and its

people. One work, *The Ugly Face of Occupation*, is a photomontage of Iraqi people in the shape of a ziggurat. On the top of the temple, a model of a coalition tank drips blood on the images of the people. Another of his powerful works, *Mission of Destruction*, is a 45-foot-long (14 m) mural showing acts of war and the destruction of Azzawi's homeland.

Azzawi has not been back to Iraq since 1980. "But my concern," he says, "is still Iraq and that part of the world."

For thousands of years, sculpture has been a dominant art-form in Iraqi culture. Jawad Selim, who for a time served as the head of the sculpture department at the Institute of Fine Arts, is best known for his *Liberty Monument* located in Baghdad's Tahrir Square. The monument celebrates the people of Iraq

Iraq's strong tradition of modern art is apparent in Jawad Selim's *Liberty Monument* in Baghdad.

and the 1958 revolution, which overthrew the monarchy of King Faisal II. Selim's sister, Naziha Selim, was one of Iraq's most prominent modern sculptors. Jalal Talabani, president of Iraq from 2005 to 2014, called her "the first Iraqi woman who anchored the pillars of Iraqi contemporary art."

One of the greatest architects of modern times, Zaha Hadid, was born in 1950 into a prominent family in Baghdad. She attended college in Lebanon and England, and eventually set up her architecture firm in London. Hadid, who died in 2016, was known for her bold, geometric designs. Her swooping shapes and fragmented blocks consistently attracted attention and praise. In 2004, she became the first woman to be awarded the Pritzker Architecture Prize, the world's top honor for architects.

A Museum Returns

Iraq's finest collection of art and ancient artifacts is housed in the National Museum of Iraq in Baghdad. The collection contains thousands of pieces dating to the great Mesopotamian civilizations of Sumer, Babylonia, and Assyria.

Since the 2003 invasion, the museum has suffered many hardships. After Baghdad fell to U.S. forces in April 2003, looters stole about fifteen thousand objects from the museum. During the two-day ransacking, professional art thieves made off with some of the collection's most treasured items. Among the stolen items were bronze and stone statues, pottery, ivories, and jewelry. Many looters simply destroyed objects on site.

A team of Federal Bureau of Investigation (FBI) agents, U.S. soldiers, and United Nations workers was formed to help track down and recover the stolen items. Its members sent descriptions of the stolen goods to border guards, international police departments, and archaeologists around the globe. Within weeks, stolen items began to return. Some objects were found hidden in people's homes, and others were tracked down on the black market. Some items simply showed up at other museums.

About half of the stolen treasures have been returned or located for safekeeping. After being closed for nearly twelve years, the museum was officially reopened to the public in February 2015.

Literature

Early Iraqi literature has been enjoyed around the globe for centuries. One of the world's most popular myths is the *Epic of Gilgamesh*, which dates back to ancient Sumeria. The epic poem follows the adventures of King Gilgamesh of Uruk, an ancient city of Sumer, on his quest for immortality. Some people believe the biblical story of Noah and the great flood is based on a flood that occurs in the tale of Gilgamesh.

The stories in the *Epic of Gilgamesh* were discovered on ancient stone tablets, some dating back as far as 2100 BCE.

One Thousand and One Nights is a collection of stories from Arab, Turkish, Greek, and Indian sources. Scholars believe the stories originated as oral tales before the eighth century CE. In the following two centuries, people in what is now Iraq added Arab stories, and more Middle Eastern stories were added in later years. "Aladdin's Lamp," "Ali Baba and the Forty Thieves," and "The Seven Voyages of Sinbad" are but a few of the familiar tales that appear in the collection.

Some of Iraq's best-known literary figures are poets. Born in Basra to a date grower and shepherd, Badr Shakir al-Sayyab is said to be one of the most influential Arab poets of all time. His book of poems, *Rain Song* (1960), is a classic in Arabic literature, incorporating traditional Iraqi folklore and political and social themes.

While in prison as a political foe of Saddam Hussein's regime, Salah Al-Hamdani began writing poetry. His 2003 poem "Baghdad My Beloved" speaks of his self-imposed exile from Iraq and his opposition to the U.S. occupation of his homeland.

Novelist Iqbal Al-Qazwini was exiled in Germany during Hussein's rise to power in 1979. Her most famous work, *Zubaida's Window*, is the story of a young Iraqi woman who flees her country to live in Europe. Through the experiences of the main character, the reader learns about the violence and instability in Iraq from the Baath takeover to the late 1980s.

Another Iraqi novelist, Ahmed Saadawi, has chosen to remain in Baghdad. He brings to life the experiences of Iraqis who have stayed, living through the American invasion of 2003 and the upheaval that followed. Saadawi's novel *Frankenstein in Baghdad* won the 2014 International Prize for Arabic Fiction.

Many of the stories included in *One Thousand and One Nights* have become known around the world, such as the adventures of Sinbad the Sailor.

In *Frankenstein in Baghdad*, Ahmed Saadawi mixes supernatural elements with the modern realities of war-torn Iraq.

Music

The music of Iraq spans all genres from traditional to classical to pop, soul, hip-hop, and rap. *Maqam* is one of the most popular and enduring styles of music played in Iraq, and across the entire Arab world. The music is played on traditional Middle Eastern instruments. Among these instruments is the *oud*, a short-neck, pear-shaped instrument. The dulcimer-like Iraqi *santur*, invented in Mesopotamia, is played by striking the strings with two sticks. The *darbuka* is a single-headed drum with a goblet-shaped body. The *ney* is a long flute played by blowing into one end.

Pop music in Iraq merges ancient musical styles and lyrics with traditional and modern instruments. Kadim al-Sahir, born in 1957, has been an Iraqi favorite for more than three decades. His first hit single, "The Snake Bite," was censored by the Iraqi government. Many of his songs feature romantic and political themes. Al-Sahir has worked with many international music celebrities, including Lenny Kravitz, Quincy Jones, and Sarah Brightman. Basra-born Seta Hagopian is a pop music icon best known for using Western instruments in her interpretations of Iraqi songs. She has performed throughout the Arab world, Europe, and Asia. Her daughter, Nova Emad, has won fame as a vocalist in Canada, Europe, and the Middle East.

Formed in 2001, Acrassicauda, Iraq's first heavy metal band, was inspired by Western groups such as Metallica, Iron Maiden, and Rage Against the Machine. Members of the band began to receive death threats from Islamic militants who accused the

The oud is a common instrument throughout much of the Muslim world. Its name comes from an Arabic word meaning "wood."

Kadim al-Sahir performs at a concert in Scotland. He has been performing internationally since the 1980s.

group of worshipping the devil. The band eventually relocated to the United States.

Classical music lovers in Iraq enjoy the performances of the Iraqi National Symphony Orchestra, formed in 1944. In 1962, the Iraqi Minister of Culture abolished the orchestra, but its members maintained the group and rehearsed secretly for eight years. In 2003, the orchestra performed with the U.S. National Symphony Orchestra in Washington, D.C.

The National Youth Orchestra of Iraq offers musicians between the ages of fourteen and twenty-nine the opportunity to train with professional American and European musicians. Sponsored by the Kurdish Regional Government, the training takes place during an intensive two-week summer camp in Kurdistan. The orchestra was founded by Iraqi pianist Zuhal Sultan in 2008.

Sports

Soccer and basketball reign as the two most popular sports in Iraq. Since the 1980s, Iraq's national soccer team has experienced numerous highs and lows, often caused by political meddling. Once a regional powerhouse, Iraq has won gold medals at the West Asian Games, the Arab Nations Cup, the Pan Arab Games, the Asian Games, and the Gulf Cup of Nations.

The team had its greatest victory in 2007, winning the Asian Football Confederation Asian Cup. Considered underdogs to win the tournament, the Iraq team—a mix of

Soccer has been popular in Iraq since the early twentieth century. British soldiers stationed in Iraq introduced the game to the region.

The Legendary Ammo Baba

Ammo Baba was born to be a soccer legend. As a young boy, he learned the ins and outs of the game as he watched British soldiers play at their base in Baghdad, his hometown. In 1955, at age twenty, he was invited to play for Iraq's national team. Two years later, he scored his country's first goal in Iraq's first official international match. During the 1950s and 1960s, Baba played for several professional teams in Iraq, as well as the national team and the Iraq military team. By then a revered national hero, Baba hung up his cleats in 1970 to begin a long and successful career as a soccer coach.

Coach Baba led the Iraq national team to Gulf Cup victories in 1979, 1984, and 1988, and an Arab Cup victory in 1988. His teams qualified for three consecutive Olympics, in 1980, 1984, and 1988. In 1984, at the height of the squad's great success, Saddam Hussein turned over control of the team to his son Uday. The new manager demanded foolish changes, broke league rules, and physically tortured players when the team lost. As a result, Iraq was banned from some international competitions. At the risk of his life and his livelihood, however, Baba ignored the younger Hussein's demands and told him he knew nothing about soccer. Uday threatened to cut out Baba's tongue or

hang him, but the coach would not give in.

"How did I survive?" asked Baba. "Because the people loved me."

Baba survived the Hussein regime, but Iraqi soccer was never the same. The national team declined throughout the 1990s and failed to win a championship until 2002. Ammo Baba, the great soccer legend who stood up against Uday Hussein, died in 2009 at the age of seventy-four.

Sunnis, Shi'ites, and Kurds—upset heavily favored Australia and South Korea before defeating Saudi Arabia 1–0 in the final game. Joyous Iraqis put aside their differences and came together to celebrate the historic win. "The players have made us proud, not the greedy politicians," said a police officer in

A growing number of Iraqi women are playing sports such as basketball.

Baghdad. "Once again our national team has shown that there is only one, united Iraq." Soccer fans also enjoy attending games played between the twenty clubs that make up the Iraqi Premier League.

Hoop fans follow their favorite basketball teams in the Iraqi Division I Basketball League. The ten-team league features squads from Baghdad, Duhok, Hillah, Najaf, Zakho, and Basra. Men's and women's teams from Iraq also compete in lesser leagues. The Iraq national basketball team competed in the 1948 Olympic Games and numerous times in the International Basketball Federation (FIBA), Asia Championship, the Pan Arab Games, and the West Asia Basketball Association Championship.

CHAPTER 10

Daily Life

THE EFFECT OF WARS AND ONGOING VIOLENCE IMPACT the daily lives of the Iraqi people. Yet as the new political system stabilizes and economic conditions improve, Iraqis remain optimistic about their future and the future of their homeland.

Family Life

The family plays the most important role in the lives of most Iraqis. Even during the country's recent upheavals, the family remained a vital social unit. Families provide protection, food, and shelter for young and old alike. In many instances, the family also furnishes income. Iraqis often have relatives as business partners because they are believed to be more trustworthy and reliable than people outside the family unit.

An elderly man in northern Iraq. The life expectancy in Iraq is seventy-three for men and seventy-seven for women.

In modern Iraq, the extended family—parents, grandparents, children, aunts, uncles, and cousins—rarely lives together as they did in past times. Despite living apart, however, relatives remain loyal to the family and continue to share the same values and goals.

The Iraqi family typically consists of a husband and wife, their sons, their son's wives, and unmarried daughters. Traditionally, the father was the head of the family and the main authority figure. In theory, he makes important decisions that affect the family, such as the children's education and the occupations they will enter. In reality, however, many mothers lead households, while fathers work outside the home.

These age-old family structures are stronger now in rural Iraq than in cities. Though families remain important to city dwellers, they often set aside traditional behaviors in favor of adopting more contemporary ways.

Children in Iraq usually live with their parents until they marry, and often even after marriage, especially if they do not have the economic means to have a house of their own.

Marriage

It is traditional in Iraq for parents to decide whom their children will marry. When selecting or approving a suitable mate

An extended family enjoys a meal together in Arbil.

The Iraqi Wedding Party

On the day of her wedding, an Iraqi bride wears a white gown and the groom a new suit. The official wedding ceremony is supervised by a judge. A reception is held after the ceremony during which time the traditional *dabkah*, a line dance, is performed. The wedding cake is cut with a sword, followed by a toast to the newlyweds. The final wedding party is the *sab'a*, which means "seven" in Arabic. Traditionally, the party would take place seven days after the wedding. Today, it is held when the couple returns from their honeymoon. The party is held at the house of the groom's family and hosted by his new wife. Only female relatives and friends may attend the party. While the party goes on, the new husband stays in a separate room of the house by himself.

for their child, parents carefully examine the family background, character, and financial standing of an individual. Young, educated Iraqis living in the cities generally select their own partners, although parents must approve the union. Young women generally marry at an earlier age than young men. Iraqi families tend be large, with four or more children being common.

Women in Iraq

Until recent years, women were discouraged from working outside the home. But as men left the workforce to join the military and fight in wars, a shortage of labor was created. For the first time, positions in government, medicine, law enforcement, business, law, and other fields were opened to women.

An Iraqi doctor at work in Kut

Today, as part of an effort to promote women's rights, 25 percent of the members of parliament must be female.

Women's new roles in Iraqi society, however, are the object of political and religious dispute. After the 2003 invasion and U.S. occupation of Iraq, conservative Muslims objected to changing ways. They demanded strict controls on women's behavior. They often harassed women who wore Western-style clothing or held jobs traditionally performed by men.

In some traditional areas, the roles and behaviors of men and women in Iraq are clearly defined. Traditionally, men and women rarely gather together in public. In some places, it is considered inappropriate for an unmarried man and an unmarried woman to be alone together, although this is less the case in urban areas, especially universities and workplaces. Public physical displays of affection are also deemed improper.

Students fill a classroom in Mosul. Few children attended school in areas where ISIS was in control, but once ISIS was forced out, the children returned to school.

Education

The Iraqi Ministry of Education oversees Iraq's educational system. Public education is free, from primary school through doctoral degrees, the most advanced university degree available. Private schools exist, but they are unaffordable to most Iraqi citizens.

Given Iraq's difficult economic conditions, teachers' salaries are low and there is a shortage of textbooks and supplies. Many parents do not send their children to school, and children often drop out at an early age. These children must often find work to help support their families.

Iraqi children enter primary school at age six and attend for six years, up to grade six. The students must pass a national exam to make them eligible to attend intermediate school.

Intermediate school includes grades seven through nine. After completing this three-year program, students take another national examination. If they pass, they can then attend a secondary or vocational school. Intermediate school students study mathematics, geography, Arabic, English, science, history, and art. Female students take additional classes in home economics.

Students attend secondary school from grades ten through twelve. General secondary schools teach liberal arts. Vocational secondary schools offer instruction in agriculture, industry, and science. Students must pass an exam to continue their education any further. If students fail the exam, they are allowed to attend school for one more year and take the exam again. If they fail the exam again, they may not continue school.

A teacher and students at a school in northern Iraq. About 80 percent of Iraqis can read and write.

In 2012, the Technical University of Baghdad held its first graduation since the American invasion in 2003. Iraqi universities have struggled in recent decades, as the conflict and chaos have damaged many facilities and caused many professors to leave the country.

Iraq has an extensive system of higher education. There are roughly twenty universities and forty-seven technical colleges spread throughout the country. Established in 1227, Mustansiriya University on the east bank of the Tigris in Baghdad is one of the world's oldest universities. The University of Baghdad is the largest university in Iraq and the second-largest Arab university. The school has an enrollment of more than twenty thousand students each year.

The years of war and sanctions have taken a heavy toll

on Iraq's education system. During the war years, money was diverted from education to fight the conflicts. United Nations sanctions prevented Iraq from importing new technologies and equipment. Many schools were damaged and looted following the 2003 invasion. Some had no libraries or laboratories, and even lacked basic sanitary facilities.

Since 2004, international efforts have tried to improve the weakened state of Iraqi education. Officials estimate that Iraq needs about nine thousand new schools. With money tight, however, the government was forced to cut its spending on education in 2017. Experts fear the decline in education will threaten future Iraqi generations for years to come.

Food in Iraq

The cuisine of Iraq blends Arab and Mediterranean foods and flavorings to create a distinct and delicious eating experience. A typical meal begins with *mezza*, a selection of small dishes eaten as appetizers. The dishes may include *turshi*, or pickled vegetables, and *baytinijan maqli*, fried eggplant with various seasonings served on grilled pita bread. Dips are served both as appetizers and to accompany a main meal. Hummus, made from mashed chickpeas, and *muhammara*, a hot pepper dip, are favorites.

Meat and fish dishes make up many entrée courses. Many are served with rice, salad, and pickles. Kebabs are grilled or broiled meats, such as lamb and beef, on a stick. *Tashrib* is a tomato-based soup made with lamb or chicken poured over broken up pieces of bread. *Tepsi baytinijan* is a casserole dish made

Iraqi Tashrib

Tashrib is a popular main course in Iraq and other places throughout the Middle East. It is tasty, nutritious, and easy to prepare. Have an adult help you with this recipe.

Ingredients

8 pieces of chicken without the skin

2 onions, finely chopped

4 garlic cloves, crushed

1 8-ounce can chickpeas, with liquid

1½ tablespoons curry powder

1/3 cup chopped coriander

salt

black pepper

1 chicken stock cube

1 8-ounce can chopped tomatoes

2 liters water

3 tablespoons tomato puree

5 medium potatoes, cut into quarters

Directions

Fry the chicken pieces in oil. Set the chicken aside. Fry the onion and garlic, and add the chickpea liquid. Add the spices. Stir in crumbled chicken stock cube, chopped tomatoes, and water. When it boils, add the tomato puree. Add the potatoes, chickpeas, and chicken. Boil until the potatoes are cooked. Serve over cut up bread or rice.

A chef prepares pastries in the city of Najaf.

with fried eggplant and chunks of meat that are then baked.

If Iraq had a national dish, it would be *masgouf*. The dish consists of a whole fish, usually carp, which is cut open, with the skin left on, and seasoned with spices. It is slow roasted for hours on an open fire. The dish is garnished with lime, chopped onions, and tomatoes, and served with bread.

For quick eating and meals on the run, Iraqis enjoy sandwiches and wraps. *Shawarma* is a pita wrap made with shaved lamb, goat, chicken, or beef. Falafel sandwiches and *lahem bi ajin*, bread stuffed with ground meat and onion, are also common.

A cook shaves off roasted meat to make shawarma.

Popular drinks include tea, which is drunk throughout the day, and a strong, bitter-tasting coffee. *Sharbat*, a chilled sweet drink made from fruit juice, and *shinena*, a beverage of yogurt and cold water, are standard hot weather drinks.

Clothing

Fashion in Iraq is a mix of traditional Arab garb and Western styles. Traditional clothing is more common in rural areas. The traditional Arab garment for men is an ankle-length, long-sleeved robe called a *dishdasha*. A pair of loose-fitting trousers is worn underneath the robe, and the head is usually covered with a wrapped scarf called a *yashmagh*. In chilly weather, men also wear a cloak called an *aba*. Traditional clothing for a woman is the *abaya*, a long, dark dress that covers the head and body and is worn over a dress or pants. Women also wear a headscarf called a *hijab*.

As many rural people have moved to the cities in recent years, more traditional clothing and a combination of traditional and modern styles are seen there. Nevertheless, many men and women in urban areas dress much like people do in the West. Women wear long pants, jeans, and short-sleeved shirts. Men sport tattoos, and wear sneakers and T-shirts. Traditional clothing is still common in most rural areas of Iraq.

Celebrations

Most celebrations in Iraq have a religious significance. The major Muslim festivals are Ramadan, Eid al-Fitr, and Eid al-Adha. Ramadan takes place during the ninth month of the Islamic calendar. During this month, Muslims fast from sunrise to sunset. Worshippers reflect on spiritual matters and bring themselves closer to God by praying more and reading the Qur'an more frequently. Each day after sundown, the family gathers for an evening meal, the *iftar*.

Older people in Iraq are more likely to wear traditional Arab clothing.

National Holidays

New Year's Day	January 1
Armed Forces Day	January 6
Labor Day	May 1
Republic Day	July 14
National Day	October 3

Iraq also celebrates several Muslim holidays. The Islamic calendar is eleven days shorter than the Western calendar. As a result, religious holidays fall on different days in the Western calendar each year.

Ras al-Sana Islamic	New Year
Mawlid al-Nabi	Prophet Muhammad's birthday
Eid al-Fitr	Celebration concluding Ramadan, the month of fasting
Eid al-Adha	Feast of the Sacrifice
Ashura	Commemoration of the martyrdom of Husayn, Muhammad's grandson

Eid al-Fitr marks the end of Ramadan. For three days, Muslims feast on special foods and tasty sweets. People wear new clothing for the joyous days of celebration, and relatives

During Eid al-Adha, many Iraqi families visit cemeteries to honor those who have died.

give children small gifts of money. Many people stay at home to spend time with family and friends. Others go to local parks to enjoy the carnival rides and horse rides specially set up for the occasion.

Eid al-Adha, the feast of the sacrifice, occurs in the twelfth month of the Islamic calendar when Muslims visit Mecca for the hajj. Muslims recount the story of Abraham that appears in the Bible and the Qur'an. In the story, God tests Abraham's faith by telling him to sacrifice his son. When God sees Abraham is willing to obey the command, he has the old man kill a lamb instead. To honor the event during Eid al-Adha, Muslims slaughter a sheep, goat, or cow. They give some of the meat to the poor and some to family members. The remaining

Many Iraqis celebrate Persian New Year, which takes place in March, at the time of the spring equinox. As part of the celebration, people in Aqrah, north of Arbil, carry torches up a mountain and then light bonfires.

meat that they keep for themselves is used to prepare a fine family feast.

Iraqis also celebrate nonreligious events. In April, Iraqi Kurds celebrate Liberation Day to mark the collapse of Saddam Hussein's regime and fall from power. Kurds also celebrate the traditional Iranian new year holiday called Nowruz, which takes place in the spring. The nation celebrates Republic Day on July 14, the day the monarchy of Faisal II was overthrown. The largest countrywide celebration is National Day on October 3, which commemorates the independence of Iraq from Great Britain in 1932.

Iraqis are a strong and resourceful people, having endured decades of horror and destruction. Though the nation's future prospects may be threatened by economic troubles, violence, and unresolved differences between ethnic and religious communities, Iraqis remain proud of their land's history as the birthplace of civilization, and they are determined to return their nation to its former glory.

Iraqis enjoy a ride at an amusement park in Baghdad. Amusement parks are popular in Iraq, and many have been built in recent years.

Timeline

IRAQI HISTORY

Ottomans join World War I on the side of the Central powers.	**1914**
The League of Nations confirms Great Britain's control over Iraq.	**1920**
Iraq becomes independent.	**1932**
The monarchy is overthrown, and Iraq becomes a republic.	**1958**
The Baath Party takes control of the Iraqi government.	**1968**
Saddam Hussein becomes president of Iraq.	**1979**
The Iran-Iraq War is fought and ends with a cease-fire.	**1980–1988**
Iraq invades Kuwait; the United Nations places economic sanctions on Iraq.	**1990**
The Iraqi army is driven out of Kuwait during the Persian Gulf War.	**1991**
A U.S.-led coalition of troops takes control of Baghdad and ousts Saddam Hussein from power.	**2003**
Iraqis vote to approve a new constitution.	**2005**
ISIS rebels attack the city of Mosul.	**2014**

WORLD HISTORY

1865	The American Civil War ends.
1879	The first practical lightbulb is invented.
1914	World War I begins.
1917	The Bolshevik Revolution brings communism to Russia.
1929	A worldwide economic depression begins.
1939	World War II begins.
1945	World War II ends.
1969	Humans land on the Moon.
1975	The Vietnam War ends.
1989	The Berlin Wall is torn down as communism crumbles in Eastern Europe.
1991	The Soviet Union breaks into separate states.
2001	Terrorists attack the World Trade Center in New York City and the Pentagon near Washington, D.C.
2004	A tsunami in the Indian Ocean destroys coastlines in Africa, India, and Southeast Asia.
2008	The United States elects its first African American president.
2016	Donald Trump is elected U.S. president.

Fast Facts

Official name: Republic of Iraq

Capital: Baghdad

Official languages: Arabic and Kurdish

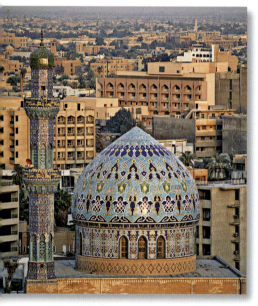

Baghdad

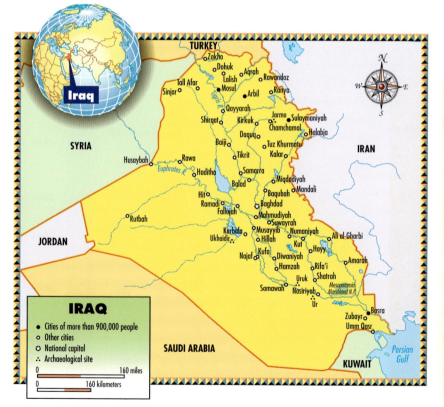

National flag

Euphrates River

Official religion:	Islam
Year of founding:	1932
National anthem:	"Mawtini" ("My Homeland")
Type of government:	Parliamentary republic
Head of state:	President
Head of government:	Prime Minister
Area:	169,235 square miles (438,317 sq km)
Longitude and latitude of geographic center:	33° N, 44° E
Bordering countries:	Turkey to the north; Iran to the east; Kuwait to the south; and Saudi Arabia, Jordan, and Syria to the west
Highest elevation:	Cheekha Dar, 11,847 feet (3,611 m) above sea level
Lowest elevation:	Persian Gulf at sea level
Average daily high temperature:	In Baghdad, 60°F (15.5°C) in January, 111°F (44°C) in July
Average daily low temperature:	In Baghdad, 39°F (4°C) in January, 74°F (23°C) in July
Average annual precipitation:	4 to 7 inches (10 to 18 cm); 2 feet (0.6 m) in mountainous regions

National Museum of Iraq

Currency

National population (2017 est.): 39,192,111

Population of major cities (2017 est.):

Baghdad	7,216,000
Basra	2,600,000
Mosul	1,739,800
Arbil	932,800
Sulaymaniyah	723,170

Landmarks:
- ▶ *Abbasid Palace,* Baghdad
- ▶ *Ali Ibn Abi Talib Shrine,* Najaf
- ▶ *Citadel,* Arbil
- ▶ *National Museum of Iraq,* Baghdad
- ▶ *Ziggurat of Ur,* Nasiriyah

Economy: Iraq's oil industry accounts for more than 90 percent of the government's revenue. The nation's leading agricultural products include wheat, barley, rice, vegetables, and dates. Factories produce chemicals, textiles, construction materials, processed foods, and leather.

Currency: The dinar (IQD). In 2017, 1,169 IQD equaled US$1.

System of weights and measures: Metric system

Literacy rate: 80%

Schoolchildren

Ammo Baba

Common Arabic words and phrases:

Sa-bah al-khair	good morning
As-sa-lam a-lay-kum	hello (peace be upon you)
Ma sa-la-ma	good-bye (with peace)
Na'am	yes
La	no
Shu-kran	thank you
Mini fad-lak	please (to a man)
Mini fad-lik	please (to a woman)
Kaif-hal-ak?	How are you?
Kum?	How much?
Is-mi . . .	My name is . . .

Prominent Iraqis:

Haider al-Abadi (1952–)
Prime minister

Dia Azzawi (1939–)
Artist

Ammo Baba (1934–2009)
Soccer player and coach

Zaha Hadid (1950–2016)
Architect

Abd al-Karim Qasim (1914–1963)
Iraqi army leader and prime minister

Kadim al-Sahir (1957–)
Singer

Ali al-Sistani (1930–)
Shi'a religious leader

To Find Out More

Books

▶ Bacher, Lindsay. *Alia Muhammad Baker: Saving a Library from War*. Mankato, MN: Child's World, 2016.

▶ Lassieur, Allison. *Ancient Mesopotamia*. New York: Children's Press, 2012.

▶ Marsico, Katie. *ISIS*. Minneapolis, MN: ADBO Publishing, 2016.

▶ Westmark, Jon. *The Iraq War: 12 Things to Know*. Mankato, MN: 12-Story Library, 2016.

Music

▶ Alhaj, Rahim. *Where the Soul Is Settled: Music of Iraq*. Washington, DC: Smithsonian Folkways, 2006.

▶ Al-Sahir, Kadim. *The Book of Love*. Abu Dhabi, UAE: Platinum Records, 2016.

▶ Visit this Scholastic website for more information on Iraq:

www.factsfornow.scholastic.com

Enter the keyword **Iraq**

Index

Page numbers in *italics*
indicate illustrations.

population of, *11*, 16, 23, 53, 73, 74

province of, 60

railways in, 71

Sunni Muslims in, *92*

Tahrir Square, 99, *100*

Technical University of Baghdad, *118*

Tigris River in, *17*, 53

University of Baghdad, 118

World War I and, 41

"Baghdad My Beloved" (Salah Al-Hamdani), 103

al-Bakr, Ahmad Hasan, 43

Baqir, Sayyid Muhammad, 93

basketball, 109, *109*

Basra. *See also* cities.

agriculture, 23

Aramaic language, 79

climate, 16

economy of, 23

manufacturing in, 68

population of, 21, 23, 73, 74

port of, 23, 71

bats, 26

baytinijan maqli (food), 119

bears, 26, *33*

Bedouin people, 75, *75*

beverages, 122

birds, 27–28, *27*

birth rates, 74

black-crowned night heron, 27, *27*

borders, 18

Bush, George W., 46, 47

C

caliphs (Muslim rulers), 39

calligraphy, 96, 97–98

caracals, *24*

carp, 28

cats, *24*, 25–26

Central Criminal Court, 60

Central Kurdish dialect, 79

Chaldean people, *78*

Cheekha Dar, 16, 20

children, *12*, *76*, *110*, 112, 113, 114, 116, *116*

Christianity, 78, 86, 92, 94, *94*

chukar partridge (national bird), 28, *28*

Circassian people, *78*

Citadel of Arbil, 23

cities. *See also* Arbil; Baghdad; Basra; Kirkuk; Mosul; towns; villages.

Amarah, *47*

Aqrah, *76*, *126*

Babylon, 10

Dohuk, 78, 79

Karbala, 78

Kufa, 39

Kut, *115*

Najaf, 78, 91, *121*

Nineveh, 23

Samarra, 78

Sulaymaniyah, 73, 79

civil war, 47

climate, 16, *17*, 18, 21–22, *22*

clothing, 87, 115, 122–123, *123*, 124

Code of Hammurabi, 37

conservation, 32–33, *33*

constitution, 47, 51, 54–55, 56, 83

construction industry, *62*, 69

Council of Ministers, 59

Council of Representatives (COR), 57, *57*, 59

cuneiform writing, 36, 97

Cyrus the Great, 38

D

darbuka (musical instrument), 104

date palms, 31, *31*, 66–67, *71*

Dawa Party, 59

Dhi Qar province, 37

dinar (currency), 64, *64*

dishdasha (clothing), 122

Dohuk, 78, 79

E

economy

agriculture, 66

Basra, 23

construction industry, *62*, 69

currency (dinar), 64, *64*

employment, 12, 47, *62*, 63, 68, 111, 114, *115*, 116

exports, 65, *65*, *71*

fishing industry, 29, 69

imports, 67

Iraq War and, 64

manufacturing, 66, 68

mining, 66

oil industry, 11, 13, 23, *42*, 63, 64–65, *65*

sanctions, 45, 64, 66, 68, 71, 119

terrorism and, 63

tourism, 26

trade, 9, 23, 36, 91

education, 10, 43, 47, 53, 68, 116–119, *116*, *118*

Eid al-Adha holiday, 125–126, *125*

elections, 50, 54

elevation, 16, 20

employment, 12, 47, *62*, 63, 68, 111, 114, *115*, 116

Epic of Gilgamesh, 101, *102*

Euphrates River, 9, *14*, 16, 17–18, *19*, 26, 30, 31, 64

executive branch of government, 42, 43, *43*, 44, *44*, 55, *55*, 56, 57, 100, 133

exports, 65, *65*, *71*

F

Faisal I (king), 41, 42

Faisal II (king), 42, 58, 100, 126

falafel (food), 121

Mecca, Saudi Arabia, 84, 85, 86, 87, 87, 125
Medina, Saudi Arabia, 85
Mesopotamia, 9–11, 35, 38, 39, 41, 78, 97
Mesopotamia Marshland National Park, 19
Mesopotamian language, 79
metalwork, 23
mezza (foods), 119
military, 41, 42, 59, 91
mining, 66
Ministry of Oil, 65
Mission of Destruction (Dia Azzawi), 99
Mongols, 40, 53, 77
Mosque of Ali, 91
mosques
    Ali Ibn Abi Talib Shrine, 91, *91*
    Al-Kadhimiya Mosque, 53
    Great Mosque of Samarra, 64
    Jalil Khayat, 96
    minaret, 85
    tilework, 82
Mosul. *See also* cities.
    Aramaic language, 79
    Armenians in, 78
    education in, *116*
    Islamic State (ISIS) in, 48
    Kurdish language in, 79
    oil industry, 23
    population of, 23, 73
    railways in, 71
Muhammad (Islamic prophet), 38, 84–85, 88, 89
music, 61, 104–106, *106*, 133
Mustansiriya University, 118

N
Nabonidus (Babylonian king), 37
Nabopolassar (Babylonian king), 37
Najaf, 78, 91, *121*

national anthem, 61
National Assembly of the Iraqi Transitional Government, 51
national bird, 28, *28*
national flag, 58, *58*, *61*
national holidays, 124, 126, *126*
National Museum of Iraq, 53, 101, *101*
national parks, 19, *33*
national soccer team, 107–109
National Youth Orchestra of Iraq, 106
Nature Iraq group, 32–33
Nebuchadnezzar II (Babylonian king), 37–38
New Year holiday, *126*
ney (musical instrument), 104
Nineveh, 23
Northern Kurdish dialect, 79
North Mesopotamian language, 79
Nowruz holiday, 126

O
oil industry, 11, 13, 23, *42*, 63, 64–65, *65*
Olympic Games, 109
One Thousand and One Nights, 102, *103*
orchard grasses, 29
Ottoman Empire, 40, 53, 78
oud (musical instrument), 104, *105*

P
people. *See also* women.
    Ajam, 78
    Akkadians, *34*
    Arabs, 23, 38, 73, 74–75
    Armenians, 23, 78
    Assyrians, 23, 37, *77*, 77–78, *78*
    Babylonians, 36
    Bedouins, 75, *75*
    birth rates, 74
    Chaldeans, 78

    children, *12*, 76, *110*, 113, 114, 116
    Circassians, 78
    clothing, 87, 115, 122–123, *123*, 124
    education, 10, 43, 47, 53, 68, 116–119, *116*, *118*
    employment, 12, 47, *62*, *63*, 68, 111, 114, *115*, 116
    families, *110*, 111–113, *113*, 124–125
    health care, 12, 43, 47, 115
    housing, 19, 36, 80, 112, 113, 114
    Kurds, 20, 23, 43–44, 52, 54, 55, *55*, *72*, 75–76, *76*, 78, 108, 126
    languages, 78–79
    life expectancy, *112*
    literacy rate, *117*
    marriage, 113–114, *114*
    Marsh Arabs, 19, *19*
    Mongols, 40, 53, 77
    population, *13*, 16, 21, 23, 53, 73, *74*
    refugees, 49, *49*, 80–81, *81*
    Sumerians, 8, 35–36
    Syrian refugees, 80–81, *81*
    Turkmen, 23, 77, *78*
    weddings, 114, *114*
    Yazidi, 78
Persian Empire, 38
Persian Gulf, 15, 23
Persian Gulf War, 37, 45, 53
Persian language, 79
Persian New Year, *126*
peshmerga militia, 76
philosophy, 41
plant life
    conservation, 32–33
    deserts, 29
    grasses, 29
    Hanging Gardens of Babylon, 38, *39*

Meet the Author

NEL YOMTOV IS AN AWARD-WINNING author who has written nonfiction books and graphic novels about American and world history, geography, science, mythology, sports, and careers. He has written numerous books in Scholastic's Enchantment of the World series, including *Scotland*, *Syria*, *Costa Rica*, *Israel*, *Russia*, and others.

Yomtov was born in New York City. He worked at Marvel Comics as a writer, editor, colorist, and director of product development. He has served as editorial director of a large children's book publisher and as publisher of the Hammond World Atlas book division. In addition, Yomtov was a consultant to Major League Baseball, where he helped develop an educational program for elementary and middle schools throughout the country.

Yomtov lives in the New York area with his wife, Nancy, a teacher. His son, Jess, is a sports journalist.

Photo Credits